YOUR INTENTIONAL FINANCIAL LIFE

YOUR INTENTIONAL FINANCIAL LIFE

A Twelve-Month Path to Clarity and Confidence

Andrew Rosen, CFP®

Diversified Publishing, Diversified LLC

The information contained in this book is for educational and informational purposes only and should not be considered financial, investment, legal, or tax advice. Readers should consult with qualified professionals before making financial decisions.

CFP® and CERTIFIED FINANCIAL PLANNER™ are certification marks owned by Certified Financial Planner Board of Standards, Inc. These marks are awarded to individuals who successfully complete the CFP Board's initial and ongoing certification requirements.

ISBN 979-8-9957757-2-0 (Hardcover)
ISBN 979-8-9957757-1-3 (Paperback)
ISBN 979-8-9957757-0-6 (eBook)

Edited by: Sarah Thomas
Cover design by: Kyriaki and Maria Maris

Printed in the United States of America

To my parents: Thank you for always believing in me and showering me with endless love. Miss you Pop-E!

To my wife Jess and my children Aviva, Emmet, Belly: You are my reason for being. Thank you for always making me better.

FOREWORD

I didn't set out to write this book.

And I certainly didn't set out to become a financial advisor.

Like many people, I thought I had my path figured out early. My father owned a business — a payphone and calling card company he built from scratch. The plan was simple: graduate college, join him, and eventually take over. Continue building what he started.

Then, during my freshman year of college, everything changed.

My father was diagnosed with cancer. Over time, the illness forced him out of the business he had spent his life building. The company didn't survive without him. The future we had imagined — both for him and for me — disappeared.

But something else happened during that time.

While the business didn't survive, my family did.

The reason wasn't luck. It wasn't timing. It wasn't chance. It was planning. My parents had made thoughtful financial decisions years earlier — decisions they hoped they would never need. Those decisions allowed them to focus on health instead of finances. They allowed our family to maintain stability during an incredibly uncertain time. They allowed us to move forward.

That experience shaped how I think about money, life, and what really matters.

Because what I saw wasn't just the power of financial planning. I saw how financial decisions influence everything else — your stress, your relationships, your health, your happiness.

I also realized something else over time.

Life rarely unfolds in a straight line.

Careers change. Families grow. Priorities evolve. Unexpected challenges arise. Opportunities appear. And throughout it all, the decisions we make — both big and small — shape the lives we ultimately live.

That's why this book exists.

Over the past 20-plus years, I've had thousands of conversations with clients about these very moments. Some were about retirement. Others were about family, careers, health, or life transitions. But almost every conversation came back to the same idea:

Living intentionally.

This book is designed to help you do exactly that.

Your Intentional Financial Life is structured as a year-long journey — one month at a time. Each chapter focuses on a different area of your financial life, paired with real-world lessons, practical ideas, and questions designed to help you reflect and take action.

Because building a meaningful financial life doesn't happen all at once.

It happens gradually. Thoughtfully. Intentionally.

This isn't a book about chasing perfection. It's a book about making better decisions over time. It's about aligning your finances with your priorities. It's about creating space for the things that matter most.

Ultimately, it's about building a life centered around Wealth, Health and Happiness.

That's the goal.

And this book is meant to help guide you there — one intentional step at a time.

HOW TO USE THIS BOOK

This book is yours. It's a guide to help you start conversations, without going deeply into each topic. If you purchased this book midyear, feel free to jump to the corresponding month and follow along from there, or start at the beginning (January, Month 1) for the full journey. There's no wrong entry point. Maybe you want to focus on a specific area that's really bothering you, that's a great place to start too. The framework begins with you so start where you feel most comfortable.

With that being said, this book was written with the order of the months in mind. The year begins with goals; not investments, not budgets, because everything else is downstream of clarity about what you want. Protect before you build. Then together we'll address the emotional side of money (September) only after you've built the financial foundation. After that we'll end with giving, because a well-designed financial life, in the end, is about what you contribute, not just what you accumulate.

Ultimately though, it doesn't matter where you start, it's that you *do* start.

PREFACE

Why should you listen to me?

It's a fair question.

There are countless books about money, investing, and retirement. Many written by talented professionals with impressive credentials. So why this one? Why me?

Because over the course of my career, I've had a unique vantage point.

I've spent my career sitting across the table from individuals and families as they navigate some of the most important moments of their lives. I've watched people transition into retirement. I've seen families welcome children and grandchildren. I've worked with business owners as they built something meaningful — and eventually stepped away from it. I've helped clients navigate uncertainty, opportunity, and everything in between.

In many ways, I've lived these moments alongside them.

I often say that I've retired a thousand times.

I've become a parent a thousand times.

I've sold businesses a thousand times.

Not personally — but vicariously, through the people I've had the privilege of working with.

When you experience these milestones repeatedly, patterns begin to emerge. You start to see what works. You see what people wish they had done differently. You learn that financial decisions are rarely just about money — they're about time, priorities, relationships, and purpose.

Over the years, I've also learned something important: the most successful people financially aren't always the happiest. And the happiest people aren't always the wealthiest.

The individuals who seem most fulfilled tend to share something else in common — they make intentional decisions. They align their finances with what matters most to them. They recognize that money is a tool, not the destination.

This book is built on those experiences.

It reflects lessons learned from decades of conversations, decisions, and life transitions. Not theory. Not academic models. Real-world insights from working with people at different stages of life — from those just starting out to those navigating retirement and beyond.

I've seen how small decisions compound over time. I've seen how thoughtful planning can create flexibility and peace of mind. And I've seen how intentional choices can help people build lives that reflect their values.

That's what this book is about.

Not just growing wealth, but building a life centered around

Wealth, Health and Happiness.

And after more than two decades of helping others navigate their financial lives, I've come to believe that the most important decisions aren't always the biggest ones.

They're the intentional ones made along the way.

YOUR INTENTIONAL FINANCIAL LIFE

A Twelve-Month Path to Clarity and Confidence

In over two decades of financial planning, I've noticed something: the people who struggle most with money rarely have an information problem. They have a clarity problem.

Over the past 20+ years, I've sat across the table from thousands of clients—families, business owners, couples beginning their journey—often talking about goals, fears, legacy, and possibility. Money is rarely the only topic. It's the thread that ties those stories together.

Here's what I've learned: most people don't have a real financial framework. They may have an app, an advisor, or some goals, but too often their choices feel reactive. They lack a sense of direction.

This book is born out of that insight. It's not a textbook, and it's not a replacement for bespoke advice. It's a conversation starter; a structured journey to help you ask better questions, clarify priorities, and shape a financial life that aligns with your values.

Why This Book Exists

People don't usually need more information; they need a place to begin. They need clarity over complexity, direction over distraction, and a process that connects their day-to-day decisions to their long-term vision.

This book will help you frame your financial life the way I'd guide a client: with clarity, intention, and a focus on what truly matters.

I didn't write this book from theory. I wrote it from twenty-plus years of sitting across the table from real people — couples scared to look at their own accounts, retirees who'd done everything right but never figured out what 'right' was supposed to feel like, families who called me six months too late. The patterns are always the same. And the fix is almost never about the money.

What You'll Find Inside

The structure is simple: a 12-month journey. Each month addresses a major financial theme—from goals and foundation to investing, retirement, legacy, and giving. Within each month, four weekly topics break down that theme into meaningful ideas and actions.

You can read the book linearly, dip in where you are, or revisit it over time. It's designed for flexibility.

While the book is ordered so that each chapter builds on the one before, you can certainly skip around to find the one that speaks to you and where you are in your journey right now. Overall, the flow of this book starts with your goals and foundation, and ends with learning how to give and plan for the following year.

What This Book Is (And Isn't)

This is not the final answer to every question in finance. It's not a substitute for a trusted advisor. What it *is* is a structure to help you engage thoughtfully—with clarity over ego, direction over noise.

A Note On Internal Revenue Service Limits

Annual gift exclusions, lifetime estate and gift tax exemptions, 529 plan contribution rules, and Qualified Charitable Distribution limits change periodically. Instead of relying on fixed numbers that may quickly become outdated, always check the IRS website (IRS.gov) or speak with your advisor for the most current amounts.

JANUARY - MONTH 1

Financial Goals & Balance

You can have anything you want, but not everything you want.

That's a truth I've come to see clearly over more than 20 years of sitting across the table from people trying to make good financial decisions. Many of them had the right intentions and the willingness to plan, but they lacked a clear framework. They were overwhelmed by all the things they felt they *should* do, without the clarity to know what they *needed* to do.

That's why we're starting with balance.

This month is about defining what matters most to you, understanding the real trade-offs involved in financial decision-making, and beginning to align your time, money, and energy with your values.

You can have anything you want—but not everything at once. And that's okay. Planning isn't about doing more. It's about making better choices with what you have.

WEEK 1

You Can't Plan Without A Vision

You can't hit a target you can't see. I think of a client I'll call Mark — a successful surgeon who came in saying he wanted to retire at 55 with 'enough to travel.' Three conversations in, we realized what he actually wanted was to stop operating and start teaching. The number was never the point. The permission was.

Many people dive into budgeting, saving, or investing without first asking: *Where am I actually trying to go?* Without that clarity, it's easy to get stuck in cycles of stress or comparison.

Your financial plan should start with your vision. What kind of life do you want to live? Who do you want to support? What experiences matter most to you?

Start by asking yourself:

- If I had total financial freedom, how would I spend my time?
- What's most important to me over the next one to three years?
- What does "success" mean to me—personally, not just financially?

Don't worry about making your vision perfect or permanent. Your goals can (and will) evolve. What matters is starting with something that's truly yours, not borrowed from someone else's definition of success.

Action Step:

Write down three to five life goals or priorities. These are not "to-dos"—they are themes or outcomes you want to work toward over the next few years.

WEEK 2

Understanding Trade-Offs—The Theory Of Unlived Reality

Every financial decision comes with a trade-off. Every goal you pursue means there's another one put on hold. That's not a failure. It's simply reality.

We're conditioned to believe we can "have it all," but time, money, and energy are finite. Trying to do everything at once often leads to burnout, indecision, and guilt.

This week is about recognizing the power of focus.

The Theory of Unlived Reality reminds us that for every path we choose, others remain unexplored. In your financial life, this means:

- Saving for early retirement might mean postponing a dream vacation.
- Paying off your mortgage might limit how much you invest.
- Helping your kids through college might require delaying other goals.

Instead of avoiding trade-offs, plan for them. Choose them. Let your values guide which path matters most right now.

Action Step:

Identify two competing goals or priorities. What would it look like to intentionally prioritize one? What would you be giving up—and what would you be gaining?

WEEK 3

Finding Your Budgeting Style—Tight Tracker Or Big-Picture Thinker?

Budgeting is personal. Some people love tracking every expense down to the penny. Others just want to know they're on track without getting into the weeds.

Both approaches can work—but only if you choose the one that fits your personality and lifestyle.

This week is about identifying your *budgeting style* and creating a system that works for you.

Here are a few common styles:

1. **The Tracker:** You love spreadsheets or apps and want to see exactly where your money goes.
2. **The Automator:** You prefer to set up automatic savings and bills, then check in periodically.
3. **The Big-Picture Thinker:** You focus on percentages (e.g., 50/30/20) and broader goals, not daily details.
4. **The Visual Spender:** You use envelopes, buckets, or categories to manage spending behaviorally.

There's no best method, only the best one *for you*.

Action Step:

Take 10 minutes to reflect on how you naturally manage money. Then, choose one budgeting style to try (or refine) this month. The goal isn't perfection—it's consistency.

WEEK 4

Balancing Saving And Living Today

It's easy to swing too far in either direction—either saving everything and feeling deprived, or spending freely and avoiding the future.

But the most sustainable plan is one that balances both.

I'll be honest with you: I'm not naturally wired for balance. I'm wired for more. But I've watched too many clients sprint toward a number and arrive too tired to enjoy it. That's taught me something.

Saving gives you freedom later. Spending with intention gives you joy now. A good financial life includes both, and it's different for everyone.

Here are a few strategies for balancing:

- **Reverse Budgeting:** Save first (based on goals); spend what's left guilt-free.
- **Percentage Rules:** Allocate a set percentage (e.g., 20–30%) toward experiences and enjoyment.
- **Seasonal Planning:** Build in splurges or upgrades at intentional times (e.g., vacations, holidays) so they feel earned, not impulsive.

The point isn't to sacrifice joy for security—or vice versa. It's to live in a way that reflects your values *today*, while also protecting your *tomorrow*.

Action Step:

Write down one way you'll prioritize living today (a small upgrade, experience, or indulgence) *and* one way you'll commit to future savings this month.

Wrapping Up January

Clarity is the first gift of planning. By aligning your goals, values, and financial behaviors, you've taken a powerful step toward confidence and control.

Next month, we'll focus on protecting what you're starting to build—and making sure your foundation can weather life's unexpected turns.

Client Convos: Finding Goals and Balance

A client — I'll call him Zach — came in telling me the same thing over and over: he wanted to retire early. That was the goal. That was all he could talk about. But I kept pushing back. I kept asking him: retire to what? What are you retiring for?

Eventually, after several conversations, the real answer came out. Zach wanted to go back to school, get his PhD, and become a professor. Retirement wasn't the destination — it was the vehicle. What he actually wanted was the financial freedom to pursue an encore career in something he was deeply passionate about.

The planning process didn't just build a financial plan. It helped Zach discover what he actually wanted from his life. That's the difference between checking boxes and building something intentional. We weren't planning for retirement. We were planning for his next chapter.

FEBRUARY - MONTH 2

Building Your Financial Foundation

You've set your goals. You've clarified your values. Now it's time to protect what you've begun building.

This month is about creating a stable financial base, one that can absorb the unexpected and support your long-term vision. In twenty-plus years of practice, I've never once had a client tell me they built too big an emergency fund. I've heard the other version many times. The foundation isn't the exciting part of financial planning — but it is the only part that matters when life decides to test you.

Life will throw curveballs. Planning for them is not pessimistic—it's practical. Emergencies don't schedule themselves, but you *can* prepare your response in advance.

A strong foundation gives you confidence. It allows you to take calculated risks, pursue big goals, and sleep better at night knowing you're not one flat tire or medical bill away from financial stress.

This chapter focuses on:

- Building your emergency fund
- Preparing for "what-ifs" through insurance and smart safeguards
- Understanding risk and how to manage it like an adult

- Creating a system that brings peace of mind

This isn't the most glamorous part of financial planning—but it might be the most important. Wealth is built on stability, not just ambition.

WEEK 1

Three-To-Six-Months Emergency Fund Basics

If you lost your job tomorrow, how long could you keep paying your bills without stress?

An emergency fund is your buffer against the unexpected—job loss, medical expenses, home repairs, car breakdowns. It's not an investment. It's not meant to grow. Its only job is to *be there* when you need it most.

The general rule of thumb is to save **three to six months' worth of essential expenses** in an accessible, low-risk account. Essential expenses mean:

- Rent or mortgage
- Utilities
- Groceries
- Insurance
- Minimum debt payments
- Basic transportation

If your job is unstable, your income varies, or you're the sole earner in your household, aim for closer to six months of expenses. If you have dual incomes or secure employment, three months may be sufficient.

Where Should It Go?

- A **high-yield online savings account** is ideal—this earns more interest than a traditional bank account while keeping your money accessible.
- Avoid tying your emergency fund up in investments or retirement accounts.

- The money should be liquid and accessible within one to two days.

Common Barriers:

- *"I'll start saving when I make more"* → Start small. $500 is better than nothing.
- *"I don't want to keep that much cash"* → That's the point. It's not for growth; it's for protection.
- *"I'll just use a credit card if something happens"* → That's not a plan; that's debt.

An emergency fund isn't exciting. But you'll be amazed at how much calmer life feels when you know it's there.

Action Step:

Calculate your minimum monthly essential expenses. Multiply by three or six to set a goal amount. Open a separate savings account and automate monthly contributions—even if it's just $50 to start.

WEEK 2

Protection Planning—Insurance & What-Ifs

It's easy to put off thinking about worst-case scenarios. But the truth is, a strong financial plan isn't just about growing wealth. It's about protecting it.

Protection planning is the safety net that catches you when life doesn't go according to plan. Think of it as your financial seatbelt. You hope you never need it, but if you do, it can be life-changing.

This week is about preparing for those "what-if" moments—so that one accident, illness, or unexpected event doesn't derail everything you've worked toward.

Here Are The Essentials:

1. Health Insurance

Even a short hospital stay can cost thousands. Make sure you understand your deductible, your out-of-pocket max, and what your plan actually covers. If you're between jobs, consider COBRA or marketplace options. Skipping coverage is not worth the risk.

2. Life Insurance

If someone relies on your income—spouse, children, aging parents—you likely need life insurance. Term insurance is typically the most cost-effective option. A general rule: aim for 20 times your annual income in coverage.

3. Disability Insurance

Your income is your greatest asset, especially in your working years. Disability insurance protects that income if illness or injury prevents you from working. Many people have this through work but don't know what it covers. Check your policy. If you're self-employed, look into private coverage.

4. Homeowners/Renters Insurance/ Vehicle Insurance

It's not just about your stuff—homeowners or renters insurance also protects against liability (someone getting injured on your property, for example). Renters often overlook this, but it's usually inexpensive and provides major peace of mind. If you own a vehicle, you'll need vehicle insurance in order to operate it.

5. Umbrella Insurance

This kicks in after your primary policies (like auto or home) max out. If you're sued or held liable for an accident, umbrella coverage can protect your savings and future earnings. It's surprisingly affordable and often overlooked.

6. Long Term Care Insurance

Long-term care insurance is designed to help cover the cost of care if you need assistance with daily activities such as bathing, dressing, or managing medications due to aging, illness, or injury. Many people assume Medicare will cover these costs, but in most cases, it does not cover extended long-term care. Without a plan, families often find themselves paying out of pocket or relying on loved ones for care.

Protection planning isn't just about buying policies; it's about reducing risk. It's about asking: *What would happen if ...?* and then making sure the answer isn't financial disaster.

Action Step:

Review your current insurance policies. Are there any gaps? Do you understand what's covered—and what's not? Make a list of any coverage you need to research or revisit.

WEEK 3

How To Handle Risk Like A Grown-Up

Risk is unavoidable. The question isn't whether you'll face it—it's how well you'll prepare for it.

Most people misunderstand risk. They either try to avoid it completely, which leads to missed opportunities, or they ignore it, assuming nothing bad will happen. Neither approach is sustainable.

Mature financial planning means developing a healthy relationship with risk: understanding what you can control, accepting what you can't, and building a system to manage the uncertainty in between.

What Are The Real Risks?

It's not just about market downturns. Real-life financial risks include:

- Job loss or reduced income
- Major health expenses
- Unexpected home or car repairs
- Disability or death of a household income earner
- Lawsuits or legal liabilities
- Natural disasters
- Outliving your money

Most of these aren't "if" scenarios—they're "when."

The goal isn't to eliminate risk. It's to plan for how you'll absorb it when it happens.

Key Strategies For Managing Risk

1. **Diversify:** Don't rely on one income stream, investment, or strategy. Diversification is protection.
2. **Insure smartly:** We covered this last week, but insurance is one of the cheapest ways to manage major financial risk.
3. **Build margin:** Having cash reserves and living below your means gives you space to absorb surprises.
4. **Avoid over-leverage:** Debt magnifies risk. If something goes wrong, leverage can turn a small problem into a big one.
5. **Run "what-if" scenarios:** Ask yourself: if the unexpected happened tomorrow, what would I wish I had prepared?

Real-World Example

One of my clients was a successful business owner with significant income—but all of it was tied to one industry and one product. When a competitor disrupted the market, my client's revenue dropped by 70% in six months. He called me from a parking lot, hands shaking, to tell me.

My job that day wasn't to run numbers. It was to remind him that we'd already run them — months before — and that the plan was holding. Because we had already planned for diversification, contingencies, and an emergency fund, it was difficult, but survivable.

It's not about expecting the worst. It's about being able to *handle* the worst without losing everything.

Action Step:

List the top three risks you worry about most. Then, for each one, write down one thing you could do to reduce or prepare for that risk, financially or otherwise.

This is how you move from reacting to planning.

WEEK 4

Confidence In Chaos—Planning For The Unexpected

Planning isn't about predicting the future. It's about increasing your ability to adapt when the unexpected happens.

Emergencies. Job changes. Illness. Family issues. Market downturns. These are not outliers—they're part of life. What separates the financially resilient from the vulnerable isn't luck or wealth. It's preparation.

This week, we shift from technical tools to mindset. Because at some point, your plan will meet reality. And when it does, your ability to stay grounded and respond thoughtfully will make all the difference.

What Makes Chaos Manageable?

1. **Clarity on Priorities**
   When everything feels urgent, it's easy to panic. But when you've already clarified your core goals and values (like we did in January), it becomes easier to focus on what truly matters—even in the middle of uncertainty.
2. **Flexible Financial Systems**
   Automation, cash reserves, and simple planning frameworks give you the ability to pivot. Flexibility beats complexity every time.
3. **Contingency Thinking**
   Great planners think ahead. Ask yourself:
    - What would I do if I lost my job tomorrow?
    - What if the stock market dropped 30%?

- What if I needed to care for a family member unexpectedly?

You don't need detailed answers for everything, but sketching out possibilities helps reduce fear when unexpected challenges arise.

4. **Calm Beats Control**
   Many people try to create plans that prevent all risk. That's impossible. The real goal is to *build confidence* in your ability to respond—financially, emotionally, and practically.

Building A Personal Crisis Plan

Here's a simple structure to use:

- **Trigger event**: Identify what you're planning for (job loss, major expense, illness).
- **Immediate actions**: What would you need to do in the first 48 hours?
- **Financial resources**: Where would money come from (emergency fund, insurance, family)?
- **Communication**: Who would need to be contacted (spouse, advisor, employer)?
- **Recovery strategy**: What would you do to get back on track?

Writing this down—even briefly—gives you a plan you can act on instead of freezing in fear.

Action Step:

Choose one life event that would cause serious disruption. Write a one-page response plan: who you'd call, what resources you'd tap into, what steps you'd take next.

This isn't about doom and gloom—it's about confidence.

When the world shakes, you'll know your foundation is solid.

Wrapping Up February

Now you've laid the foundation: You've protected what matters, prepared for emergencies, and given yourself a sense of control —without needing to control everything.

You're not just building wealth. You're building resilience.

Next month, we'll dive into **budgeting and spending** with strategies to create a system that works for your real life, not someone else's idea of what's "ideal."

Client Convos: When The Foundation Holds

A husband and wife had been clients for years. They had done everything right — proper insurance coverage, assets titled correctly, estate planning in order, beneficiaries updated. It was a complete, well-structured financial foundation.

Then the husband passed away unexpectedly. He had been the primary breadwinner and had also managed most of the household finances. In an instant, his wife was navigating grief and the entire weight of their financial life at the same time.

But here's what I witnessed: because the foundation was already in place, we could step in immediately. There were no gaps, no scrambling, no emergencies on top of an already devastating loss. It didn't eliminate the pain — nothing does. But it meaningfully reduced the chaos. That's what real planning does. It shows up for you when life doesn't go according to plan.

MARCH - MONTH 3

Budgeting & Spending

If February was about protection, March is about intention.

Most people think budgeting is about restriction: cutting back, depriving yourself, pinching pennies. But a good budget isn't about what you *can't* do. It's about what you *want* to do—and creating a system to get there.

This month is focused on spending with purpose. Not guessing. Not winging it. But knowing what comes in, knowing what goes out, and making sure those dollars are aligned with what matters most to you.

We'll Walk Through:

- Where your money actually goes (and how to find out)
- How to reverse-budget: prioritize goals first, not last
- Common spending rules of thumb that work—and what to do when they don't
- Guilt-free spending in the context of your full financial picture

This isn't about creating the "perfect" spreadsheet. It's about building a realistic system you can live with—and stick to.

WEEK 1

What's Coming In & Where It's Going

Before we create a plan, we need a clear picture. That starts with your **cash flow**: money in and money out.

You might think you know where your money goes. But until you track it, you're guessing. And in personal finance, guessing leads to stress, debt, and missed opportunities.

Step 1: Know Your Income

- What is your **net income** each month? This is your income *after* taxes, benefits, and retirement contributions.
- Include all sources: salaries, bonuses, side gigs, rental income, child support—anything consistent.

Step 2: Track Your Spending

- Pull the last two to three months of bank and credit card statements.
- Use a tool like Monarch, YNAB, or just a spreadsheet.
- Break your spending into categories like:
    - o Housing
    - o Utilities
    - o Transportation
    - o Food (groceries + dining out)
    - o Insurance
    - o Debt payments
    - o Savings/investments
    - o Entertainment
    - o Travel

o Subscriptions

Yes, this takes time. But it will likely be one of the most eye-opening financial exercises you ever do.

Step 3: Calculate Your Surplus Or Deficit

Once you have your income and expenses:

- Subtract your total expenses from your income.
- If the number is positive, great—you have a surplus to work with.
- If it's negative, don't panic. This process is about awareness and improvement, not judgment.

Tip: Don't try to change anything this week. Just observe. The goal is clarity, not perfection.

Action Step:

Gather your last two to three months of financial data and complete a full spending review. Categorize every dollar. This is your financial MRI—it shows what's really going on under the surface. Most people expect to find a big leak. What they usually find instead is fifty small ones — subscriptions they forgot, habits that became invisible, spending that stopped feeling like a choice.

WEEK 2

Reverse Budgeting—Paying Yourself First

Most budgets start with expenses: rent, groceries, gas, and everything else that demands your attention. Then—if there's anything left—you save and invest.

That's backwards.

Reverse budgeting flips the process. Instead of saving what's left after spending, you spend what's left after saving.

The Core Concept:

Income – Non-Negotiable Goals = Lifestyle Spending Leftover

Not the other way around.

You define your savings and investing goals first—retirement, emergency fund, college, down payment—and treat those like non-negotiables. Then you build your lifestyle around what's left.

This is how wealthy people build financial freedom. Not by depriving themselves, but by prioritizing their future as much as their present.

Why It Works

- **It makes saving automatic.** You're not relying on willpower or waiting for "extra" money to appear.
- **It aligns your money with your values.** If your goal is financial independence, shouldn't your budget reflect that?

- **It reduces guilt.** When you've already funded your goals, you can spend the rest without second-guessing.

How To Start Reverse Budgeting

1. **Set Your Goals**
    - Emergency fund? Retirement? Vacation? College?
    - Assign dollar amounts and timelines to each
2. **Automate Your Contributions**
    - 401(k), IRA, Roth IRA
    - High-yield savings for short-term goals
    - Investment accounts for long-term goals
3. **Make Savings the First Bill You Pay**
    - Just like your rent or mortgage
    - Use direct deposit or auto-transfers the day after payday
4. **Spend What's Left Guilt-Free**
    - When your goals are handled, your lifestyle spending becomes a conscious choice—not a financial threat

Example:

Let's say you take home $6,000/month.

- You decide to:
    - Contribute $750 to your 401(k)
    - Save $250 to a vacation fund
    - Invest $500 in a brokerage account
    - That's $1,500 total toward goals

You build your life around the remaining $4,500. Not the full $6,000. That's reverse budgeting.

Action Step:

Choose one savings or investing goal. Set a monthly target and automate it. Even $25 is a win. Your budget now starts with your future, not your bills.

WEEK 3

Budgeting Frameworks, Stats & Rules Of Thumb

Let's face it: Most people don't love tracking every dollar. That's why systems and shortcuts matter.

This week is about giving you practical frameworks you can actually follow. No perfection required—just enough structure to keep your spending aligned with your goals.

Common Budgeting Rules That Actually Work

1. The 50/30/20 Rule (Popularized By Elizabeth Warren)

- **50% Needs:** Housing, food, utilities, transportation, insurance
- **30% Wants:** Travel, restaurants, hobbies, entertainment
- **20% Savings:** Retirement, investments, emergency fund, debt repayment

This is a great starting framework. It offers flexibility while ensuring savings are prioritized.

2. The 80/20 Rule (Pareto Principle)

Focus on the 20% of spending that causes 80% of your financial stress—or sabotages your goals. For many people, this might be:

- Dining out
- Amazon/impulse purchases

- Unused subscriptions
- Overcommitting to travel or gifts

You don't need to cut everything. Just control the things that make the biggest difference.

3. The Reverse Budget (From Week 2)

This system works well for people with predictable income who prefer simplicity. You "pay yourself first" (savings and investing) and then freely spend what's left.

Stats That Put It All In Perspective

- The average American spends nearly **$3,500/year on dining out**.
- Subscriptions add up—**over $200/month** on average.
- Nearly **60% of Americans live paycheck to paycheck**, including many high earners.
- A $100/month subscription = $36,000 over 30 years (invested at 7%).

These aren't meant to scare you—they're meant to show how small habits add up over time.

Other Useful Guidelines

- **Housing:** Try to keep it under 28–30% of take-home pay.
- **Transportation:** Costs should be no more than 15% of take-home pay.
- **Emergency Fund:** Save 3–6 months of essential expenses.
- **Life Insurance:** Get a policy that's 20 times your annual income.
- **Saving Rate:** Aim for 15–25% of income (higher if you're starting late).

Why Budgeting Fails (And How To Avoid It)

- **Too strict?** → You'll rebel
- **Too vague?** → You'll overspend
- **Too complicated?** → You'll quit

Choose a budgeting method that fits your personality, not someone else's spreadsheet. Whether you're detail-oriented or big-picture focused, there's a version that works for you.

Action Step:

Pick one framework—like 50/30/20—and run your numbers through it. Are you spending too much in one category? Can you make one change that aligns better with your goals?

WEEK 4

Guilt-Free Spending & Living Within Your Values

You don't need to feel guilty every time you buy a coffee, take a vacation, or upgrade your phone.

A great budget doesn't eliminate spending—it gives you permission to spend on what truly matters.

This week is about getting your spending and your values in sync. Because when your money is aligned with your priorities, budgeting feels less like sacrifice—and more like freedom.

Why We Feel Guilt Around Spending

- We don't know if we *can* afford it.
- We haven't defined what "enough" looks like.
- We compare ourselves to others.
- We're trying to use money to solve emotional problems (boredom, stress, concern over status).

The goal isn't to eliminate all spending. It's to **spend without regret.**

Values-Based Spending

Take a moment to reflect:

What are the top three things you value most in life?
Examples: time with family, health, freedom, creativity, personal growth, travel, community

Now look at your budget. Does your spending reflect those values?

If it doesn't, your money isn't working for you—it's just moving through you.

Creating A Guilt-Free Spending Plan

1. **Fund your goals first**
    - Retirement, debt, emergency fund, college
    - Once those are covered, you have clarity about what's "left"
2. **Define your "fun budget"**
    - This is for wants, not needs
    - Dining out, hobbies, shopping, experiences
    - Having a defined amount makes it easier to say "yes" without overthinking
3. **Give yourself permission to enjoy your money**
    - You've earned it
    - You're building a plan
    - You don't need to feel guilty when your actions match your priorities

Try The "Joy Audit"

Every year I do this myself. Each year I find at least one category where my spending and my values have quietly drifted apart. It takes twenty minutes and it never stops being useful.

Go through your recent discretionary spending and ask:

- Did this bring me joy or value?
- Would I spend that money again?
- Was it a "hell yes" or an impulse?

Cut what doesn't matter. Keep what does.

Final Thought

Financial discipline isn't about being frugal for frugality's sake. It's about building a life you're proud of—on purpose.

If your values include generosity, budget for giving. If they include rest, budget for a vacation. If they include creativity, budget for classes or supplies.

The best budget is the one that lets you live your values without stress or shame.

Action Step:

Write down your top three spending categories that bring you joy. Then list one to two areas where you could cut back without missing it. Shift money from the latter category to the former. Spend less on noise. More on meaning.

◆ ◆ ◆

Wrapping Up March

You've moved from guessing to knowing. By understanding where your money goes and creating a system that works for your life, you've built one of the most underrated financial skills there is: intention.

Next month, we tackle two topics most people avoid — death and taxes. Not the most comfortable subjects, but planning for them is one of the most powerful things you can do for the people you love.

Client Convos: Budgeting & Spending

A husband and wife came in frustrated. Every month they ran a deficit. They were both professionals, earning good incomes — and they couldn't figure out where the money was going.

The answer was simpler than they expected: they weren't running their finances as a team. Each was managing their own spending independently, with no real unified picture of what the household was actually doing with its money.

When we sat down and did a full budget analysis together, the numbers told the story. They were genuinely shocked by what they found — the amount going to dining out, to wine, to subscriptions they'd forgotten about. It wasn't that any single category was outrageous. It was the sum of a hundred small decisions made without coordination. Getting on the same page — literally sitting down together and looking at the same numbers — changed everything for them.

APRIL - MONTH 4

Death & Taxes

Benjamin Franklin famously observed that only two things in life are certain: death and taxes. Two-and-a-half centuries later, that's still the truest thing in financial planning.

Morbid? Maybe. But also essential.

This month, we face two topics that many people avoid: **estate planning** and **tax strategy**. They're often overlooked until it's too late. But when planned for in advance, they can protect your family, preserve your wealth, and reduce future stress, conflict, and cost.

Estate planning isn't just for the ultra-wealthy. If you own a home, have kids, or care about what happens to your money, you need a plan.

Tax planning isn't about evasion or trickery. It's about being efficient—keeping more of what you've earned by making smart, legal decisions.

April is about **protection, preparation, and peace of mind**.

I became more than an advisor on this topic the day I lost my father. The documents were in order. The conversations had happened. And I cannot overstate the difference that made — not financially, but emotionally — for our family in those first impossible weeks. I write this chapter from both sides of that table.

You'll Learn:

- What happens if you don't create a will (hint: it's messy)
- What documents every adult should have in place
- How to structure your estate to reflect your values
- Ways to reduce your tax burden now *and* in the future
- The connection between planning today and reducing chaos tomorrow

It's not about fear. It's about **clarity**. When you plan for what's inevitable, you take control of the outcome. And that's one of the most powerful financial decisions you can make.

WEEK 1

What Happens If You Don't Plan?

If you don't have an estate plan, don't worry—you already have one.

It's called **probate**. And it's dictated by the state you live in, not by you.

When someone dies without a will or legal instructions, their assets go through the probate process. That's the court-supervised way of distributing your estate. Sounds orderly? Not always. In fact, it can be slow, expensive, and emotionally draining for your loved ones.

What Happens In Probate

- **The courts decide who gets what.** Their decision might not match your wishes.
- **The process can take months (sometimes over a year).**
- **It's public.** Anyone can see the details of your estate.
- **It costs money.** Legal fees and court costs can eat up your estate.
- **It can create family tension.** Without clear guidance, emotions—and disputes—can run high.

Why People Avoid Planning

- "I don't have enough money to worry about that."
- "It's too complicated."
- "I'll get around to it eventually."

The truth? Estate planning isn't just about money. It's about

avoiding chaos. It's about making life easier for the people you love when they'll need it most.

What's At Risk Without A Plan

- **Minor children** could end up with guardians you didn't choose.
- **Partners or stepchildren** might be excluded from inheriting anything.
- **Business ownership** could be thrown into legal limbo.
- **Assets** may be sold or divided in ways that don't reflect your intentions.

Planning doesn't take long. But not planning can have long-lasting consequences.

Don't Wait For A Wake-Up Call

Estate planning is one of those things most people ignore—until they experience a family member's passing or medical emergency. Then the importance becomes painfully clear.

Let this chapter be your moment to take action *before* you're forced to.

Action Step:

Make a list of the people and things you care about—your family, your home, your business, your values. Ask yourself:

"If something happened to me tomorrow, would they be protected?"

If the answer isn't a clear yes, it's time to start planning.

WEEK 2

The Essentials—What Documents You Need And Why

Estate planning can sound intimidating, like it requires a law degree or a seven-figure net worth.

But in reality, a good estate plan is about having **a few clear documents** in place that speak for you when you no longer can. These documents make your wishes legally enforceable and reduce confusion, conflict, and costs.

Here are the **core essentials** every adult should consider:

1. Will (Last Will & Testament)

Your will outlines:

- Who gets your assets
- Who will care for minor children (if applicable)
- Who will oversee the distribution (your "executor")

Without a will → The state decides these things for you.

Pro Tip: Having a will doesn't mean you avoid probate—but a will *guides* probate. It's a critical starting point.

2. Financial Power Of Attorney

This gives someone you trust the legal authority to handle your financial affairs if you become incapacitated.

They can:

- Pay bills
- Manage investments
- Access accounts

Without this, even your spouse may face legal hurdles in managing your assets during an emergency.

3. Healthcare Proxy/Medical Power Of Attorney

This document names someone to make medical decisions on your behalf if you're unable to.

Think of it as your voice in a crisis, someone who understands your preferences and can advocate for you.

4. Living Will/Advance Directive

This spells out your wishes for end-of-life care (e.g., life support, feeding tubes, resuscitation).

It helps your family and doctors avoid second-guessing and can prevent painful disputes.

5. Beneficiary Designations

Add them to assets like:

- Retirement accounts, such as 401(k)s and IRAs
- Life insurance
- Certain bank accounts (with "Payable on Death" designation)

These pass directly to your named beneficiaries—**outside your will** and **outside of probate**.

Important: Keep these updated! They override what's written in your will.

6. Trusts (Optional But Powerful)

A **revocable living trust** can:

- Help you avoid probate

- Provide more control over how and when your assets are distributed
- Offer privacy and speed for your heirs
- Protect your heirs from lawsuits, divorce, or financial mismanagement

Trusts are especially useful for:

- Families with complex dynamics
- Property in multiple states
- Large or growing estates
- Those with charitable goals
- Those wanting to add an extra layer of protection for beneficiaries

Beyond efficiency and privacy, one of the most overlooked benefits of using a trust is protection. A properly structured trust can shield your children's inheritance from creditors, lawsuits, financial predators, and even future ex-spouses. In other words, a trust doesn't just outline who receives what — it protects the people you love from the financial risks and relationships you can't predict. For many families, this layer of protection is one of the most valuable reasons to include a trust in their estate plan.

Bonus Tip: Leave A Legacy That Speaks For You

Consider leaving behind a **letter of intent** or even a **video message**. It can provide emotional guidance, explain your decisions, and give loved ones a deeper connection to your wishes—beyond the legal paperwork.

Pro Tip: You can use a **codicil** to amend your will without rewriting the whole thing. It's a simple legal document that makes updates easy and official.

Summary: You Don't Need Everything—But You

Need Something

Your estate plan doesn't need to be perfect. It just needs to be **in place**. Even a basic will and POA can save your family stress, time, and money.

Action Step:

Check if you already have any of the above documents. Are they:

- Up to date?
- Stored in an accessible place?
- Shared with the right people (e.g., your executor or family)?

If you don't have anything in place yet, this is the week to start.

WEEK 3

How To Think About Taxes—Now And Later

Tax planning isn't just a once-a-year activity you scramble through in April.

It's an ongoing part of your financial strategy, **before, during**, and **after** your working years. The more you understand how taxes work, the more control you have over how much money you keep.

This week is about shifting from *reaction* to *intention*. Instead of just filing your taxes, you'll start **planning them**.

The Problem: Most People Think Too Small

Most people focus only on this year's tax return. They miss opportunities that affect their **lifetime tax liability**.

Here's the truth:

You can't eliminate taxes. But you *can* manage them.

Smart Tax Strategy Is About Timing

It's not just **how much** you earn, but **when** you earn it—and **when** you pay taxes on it.

This is especially true for:

- Retirement accounts
- Investment income
- Social Security
- Estate transfers

The goal is to pay taxes **efficiently** across your lifetime, not just minimize one year's worth.

Key Areas To Pay Attention To

1. Tax-Deferred Vs. Tax-Free Accounts

• Traditional IRA/401(k): Tax-deferred (you pay later)
• Roth IRA/Roth 401(k): Tax-free growth (you pay now)

Ask yourself: Would you rather pay taxes at today's rates—or tomorrow's?

2. Capital Gains

• Long-term assets (those held more than one year) are taxed at lower rates.
• Harvesting gains—or losses—can create flexibility and savings.

3. Tax Brackets & Income Management

• Can you stay in a lower bracket with smart withdrawals or conversions such as a Traditional IRA or tax location?
• Spreading income over multiple years often reduces tax pain.

4. Required Minimum Distributions

• Starting at age 73 (usually age 73 — confirm with your advisor as rules may change), you must take withdrawals from traditional retirement accounts.
• Planning ahead (such as taking advantage of Roth conversions in your 60s) can help reduce future RMD impact.

5. Charitable Giving

• Donor-advised funds (DAFs), qualified charitable distributions (QCDs), and appreciated asset donations can be tax-savvy strategies if giving is one of your values.

Why This Matters For Your Legacy

Every dollar lost unnecessarily to taxes is a dollar that **doesn't go to your family, your causes, or your retirement lifestyle**. That's the real cost of poor tax planning.

Good tax planning isn't about "beating the IRS." It's about aligning your financial decisions with your long-term goals—and keeping more of what you've earned.

Action Step:

Review your retirement accounts and tax returns. Are there opportunities to shift income, convert to Roth, or harvest capital gains this year? Talk to your advisor or CPA about long-term tax strategy, not just this year's refund.

WEEK 4

Putting It All Together—Leaving A Clean Legacy

Most people don't want to leave behind a mess.

But without a clear estate and tax plan, that's exactly what happens. Legal confusion, financial burden, family conflict—it's more common than you'd think.

This week is about **combining everything we've covered** to create a legacy that's thoughtful, organized, and aligned with your values.

What A "Clean Legacy" Looks Like

- Your wishes are clearly documented
- Your assets transfer smoothly
- Your family knows where to find what they need
- Your taxes are minimized as much as possible
- Your estate reflects your values, not just your valuables

This isn't about control—it's about care. You're creating clarity in a time that's likely to be emotional for those you leave behind.

The Most Common Estate Planning Mistakes

1. **Never getting around to it**
2. **Letting documents go outdated** (especially after major life changes)
3. **Forgetting to update beneficiaries** on retirement accounts or life insurance
4. **Leaving assets to minors without a trust**

5. **Not talking to your family about your plan**
6. **Thinking a trust isn't for you**

Have The Conversation—Before You Have To

It can feel uncomfortable, but communicating your wishes while you're alive:

- Reduces confusion
- Prevents resentment
- Shows your loved ones that this was intentional, not a scramble

Consider holding a simple family meeting or writing a letter of intent alongside your legal documents. Even a short note explaining your reasoning can make a difference.

Bonus Tip: Create A "When I'm Gone" Folder

This can be digital or physical. Include:

- Copies of your estate documents
- Contact info for your attorney, advisor, and CPA
- Account details (not passwords, just a roadmap)
- Insurance policies
- End-of-life preferences
- A personal letter to your loved ones

It's a small gift that creates enormous peace during a difficult time.

Final Thought

Legacy isn't just about what you leave behind. It's about **how you leave it**.

You don't need millions to create impact—you just need intention.

The more you prepare now, the more you protect the people you care about later.

Action Step:

Schedule time to review or draft your estate documents. Then, write down two to three things you'd want your family to know—not about your money, but about **you**. That's the start of a true legacy.

◆ ◆ ◆

Wrapping Up April

You've faced the topics most people put off — and you're better prepared for it. Whether you've updated a document, started a conversation, or simply gained clarity on what needs to happen next, that's real progress.

Next month, we shift from protection to growth — looking at how to invest with purpose, patience, and a clear sense of what you're building toward.

Client Convos: Death & Taxes

I was referred a client whose parents had recently passed away. It was a substantial estate. And there was no will.

What followed was one of the most painful things I've watched as an advisor — not because of the financial loss, though that was real, but because of what it did to the family. There were five adult children. Without clear direction from their parents, every decision became a negotiation. Every negotiation became a fight.

Hundreds of thousands of dollars went to attorneys and unnecessary taxes — money the parents had spent a lifetime building, simply evaporated. But the financial loss wasn't even the worst part. Those five siblings no longer speak to each other. A family was fractured. Not because anyone was a bad person, but because the documents weren't in place. Estate planning isn't a tax strategy. It's a gift you give the people you love most.

MAY - MONTH 5

Investing With Purpose

For many people, investing feels like a game, something you're supposed to "win." But investing isn't about beating the market or chasing the next hot stock. It's about using your money as a tool to reach your goals.

This month, we'll focus on **intentional investing**—understanding what you're investing for, how to build a portfolio that supports it, and how to stay disciplined when headlines and emotions try to throw you off track.

Because here's the truth:

You don't need to be lucky, brilliant, or glued to CNBC to be a successful investor. You need a plan, a purpose, and the patience to follow through.

You'll Learn:

- How compound interest does the heavy lifting (if you let it)
- What goes into a real investment strategy (and what doesn't)
- Why behaviors—not headlines—drive most long-term outcomes

- How to invest **for your goals**, not someone else's lifestyle or risk tolerance

May is when we zoom out and look at the big picture. This isn't about day trading or trends—it's about **building wealth on purpose**.

WEEK 1

Investing Isn't About Getting Rich Quick

Let's clear something up right away:

Investing is not the same as gambling.

It's not about "timing the market."

It's not about finding the next Tesla, crypto coin, or IPO windfall.

And it's definitely not about getting rich overnight.

True investing is **long-term**, **intentional**, and **grounded in a strategy** that reflects your goals, time horizon, and risk tolerance—not your emotions or your neighbor's hot tip.

Here's what a career in this business has taught me about investing: the people who do it best are almost always the ones who are least interested in it. They set up a plan, automate it, and go live their lives. They don't watch CNBC. They don't check their portfolio during market corrections. They're busy. And because they're busy, they're rich.

The Myth Of Fast Money

We live in a culture that glorifies overnight success.

Social media highlights millionaires made from meme stocks and crypto runs. But what you don't see is the **thousands who lost money** chasing those same dreams.

Real investing doesn't make headlines.

It's steady, patient, and kind of boring—on purpose.

Because boring investing is **what works**.

A Simple Truth: The Market Rewards Time, Not

Timing

Trying to predict short-term market moves is nearly impossible, even for professionals. But staying invested over time? That's how wealth is built.

You don't need perfect timing—you need time *in* the market.

What Successful Investors Do Differently

They:

- Have a plan before they invest a dollar
- Understand their risk tolerance and stick to it
- Diversify across different asset classes
- Ignore noise from the media and social platforms
- Invest with discipline, not emotion

They're not chasing quick wins. They're focused on **consistent progress toward long-term goals**.

The Power Of Having A "Why"

If your only investment goal is "to make money," it's easy to lose focus.

But when you invest to:

- Retire comfortably
- Pay for a child's education
- Leave a legacy
- Gain financial independence

... your strategy becomes rooted in purpose, not hype. That makes it easier to ride out downturns and avoid impulsive decisions.

Action Step:

Write down your top one to two investment goals. Not dollar amounts—*real-life outcomes*. What are you investing for? What would success look like in 10, 20, or 30 years?

That's your anchor. Everything else builds around it.

WEEK 2

The Eighth Wonder Of The World

Albert Einstein is often quoted (perhaps apocryphally) as saying:

"Compound interest is the eighth wonder of the world. He who understands it, earns it ... he who doesn't, pays it."

Whether he said it or not, the idea holds true:

Compound interest is one of the most powerful forces in personal finance.

It's not flashy. It doesn't require skill. It rewards one thing above all: **time.**

What Is Compound Interest, Really?

Put simply, it's **interest earned on interest**.

You invest money. It grows.

Then that growth earns more growth.

And it keeps going.

The longer you let it work, the more exponential the results become.

A Tale Of Three Investors

Let's say three people each invest $10,000 per year and earn an average return of **7% annually**:

- **Investor A** starts at age 25, invests $10,000 per year for **10 years**, then stops—but leaves the money invested.
- **Investor B** waits until age 35 and invests $10,000 per year for **30 years**, until age 65.

- **Investor C** starts at age 25 and continues to invest $10,000 every year until age 65—a full **40 years** of investing.

At age 65, here's what each would have:

- **Investor A:** ~$1,050,000
- **Investor B:** ~$919,000
- **Investor C:** ~$2,000,000

Investor A invested a total of $100,000.
Investor B invested $300,000.
Investor C invested $400,000.

Key Insight:

Despite investing **less money**, Investor A outperformed Investor B—because **time** did the heavy lifting. But **Investor C**, who started early *and* stayed consistent, built the most wealth by far. That's the full power of **compounding + consistency**.

This shows that starting early gives your money more time to grow—but staying the course supercharges the results.

Time > Timing

People often stress about when to invest:

"Should I wait until the market dips?"

"What if there's a recession coming?"

But in the long run, **starting sooner matters more than starting perfectly**.

Markets go up and down, but compound interest keeps working in the background.

Your Money Has A Job To Do

Think of compound interest like a team of employees. The earlier you put them to work, the more productive they become. Wait too long, and you miss the most powerful years of growth.

Every day you delay is a day you don't get back.

A Quiet Ally In Your Corner

Compounding doesn't make headlines. It won't impress at a dinner party. But give it time, and it will quietly, steadily build wealth behind the scenes.

You don't need to invest perfectly. You just need to **start**, **stay consistent**, and **stay invested.**

Action Step:

Use a compound interest calculator online. Plug in your current savings, a modest return rate (e.g., 6–7%), and your timeline. Let the math speak for itself. Then ask: **"How can I give my money more time to grow?"**

WEEK 3

Building A Real Portfolio—What Actually Goes Into An Investment Plan

When most people think about investing, they think about picking stocks, watching CNBC, or asking, "Is now a good time to buy?"

But building a real portfolio—the kind that supports your long-term goals—isn't about hot tips or timing the market.

It's about building something **intentional**, **diversified**, and **aligned with your life**, not just your latest gut feeling.

What An Investment Plan Is Not:

- A collection of random stocks your friend told you about
- Whatever's trending on financial news
- A portfolio made entirely of whatever performed best last year
- A spreadsheet you look at only when markets are down

What A Real Investment Plan Is:

- A structured mix of investments tailored to your goals
- Balanced across asset classes (stocks, bonds, cash, alternatives)
- A reflection of your **risk tolerance**, **time horizon**, and **purpose**
- Designed to work through market cycles—not just in bull markets

The Core Ingredients Of A Portfolio

1. **Stocks (Equities):**
Growth-oriented. Great for long-term goals. Volatile, but high potential.
2. **Bonds (Fixed Income):**
More stable. Provide income and lower risk. Often balance out stocks.
3. **Cash or Cash Equivalents:**
For short-term needs or emergencies. Low return, high liquidity.
4. **Alternatives (Optional):**
Real estate, commodities, or private investments. Can diversify returns but add complexity. Should make up a minimal amount of your portfolio (5-10% if at all) due to their volatility.

Know Your Risk—And Match It To Reality

Everyone loves risk when the market's up. No one wants it when the market's down.

A real investment plan starts by asking:

- How much volatility can I handle emotionally?
- How long until I need this money?
- What am I trying to accomplish?

Then, you build the portfolio **around those answers.**

The Most Important Part: Stay Invested

Even the best-designed portfolio won't work if you panic and sell every time the market dips.

A real investment plan:

- Is built to handle turbulence

- Helps you stay calm during volatility
- Gives you a roadmap for making decisions, not reacting emotionally

Action Step:

Look at your current portfolio. Do you know:

- What you're invested in?
- Why you're invested in it?
- Whether it aligns with your long-term goals?

If not, it might be time for a review—with your advisor or on your own.

WEEK 4

Behavior Beats Strategy—Why Emotions Can Derail Your Wealth

You can have the perfect portfolio. The right mix of stocks, bonds, funds, and accounts. A long-term plan, a trusted advisor, and solid returns.

And it can all fall apart because of one thing: **your emotions.**

When it comes to investing, **behavior matters more than brilliance.**

The Data Doesn't Lie

Study after study shows that **the average investor underperforms the market.** Why?

Because of poor timing decisions—buying high out of excitement, and selling low out of fear.

Markets are volatile. But investors' reactions are often more volatile.

Strategy sets the course. Behavior keeps you on it.

I got a call in March 2020 from a client who had been with us for eleven years. The market was down 30%. He wanted to move everything to cash. I asked him one question: 'Has your life changed, or just the number on the screen?' He paused. Then he said, 'Just the screen.' We didn't sell a thing.

Emotional Triggers That Derail Investors

- **Fear:** "The market is tanking—I need to get out before I lose everything."
- **Greed:** "Everyone is buying this stock. I need in now!"

- **FOMO:** "I'm missing out on big gains. I should've invested sooner."
- **Regret:** "I knew I should've done something different."

These are human reactions. But they're dangerous when they drive your money decisions.

Common Investor Biases To Watch Out For

Behavioral finance helps us understand that we're not always rational. Some mental traps to be aware of are:

- **Sunk Cost Fallacy:** Holding on to bad investments because you've "already lost so much"
- **Anchoring Bias:** Getting stuck on a certain price or outcome and ignoring new information
- **Recency Bias:** Believing recent performance will continue indefinitely
- **Overconfidence:** Assuming your instincts or "hunches" are smarter than the market

Recognizing these biases won't eliminate them—but it helps you step back and make more objective decisions.

The Key: Make Fewer Decisions, More Intentionally

Successful investors don't react to headlines. They:

- **Follow a plan.**
- **Rebalance when needed.**
- **Tune out the noise.**
- **Stay invested—even when it's uncomfortable.**

They understand that volatility is normal, and that time in the market matters more than timing the market.

Tools That Can Help You Stay Steady

- **Automated investing:** Set it and forget it.
- **Rebalancing schedules:** Keep your portfolio aligned without emotion.
- **Clear investment policy:** Write down your rules for when to buy/sell *before* emotions get involved.
- **Accountability:** A good advisor helps you stay grounded when markets (and headlines) get loud.

Your Mindset Is A Competitive Advantage

You don't need to predict the market. You just need the discipline to stay invested, trust your plan, and remember:

The market rewards patience, not panic.

Action Step:

Think about your past investing behavior.

- Have you ever sold out of fear?
- Jumped in late due to hype?
- Made a big move based on a headline?

Now ask: *What would've happened if I had just stuck with the plan?*

Commit to investing with **clarity, not emotion**, moving forward.

◆ ◆ ◆

Wrapping Up May

You've built a foundation for thinking about investing the right way — not as a game to win, but as a tool to serve your life. Discipline, patience, and a clear purpose will take you further than any hot tip ever could.

Next month, we shift from building wealth to preserving it — exploring how to know when you're ready to retire, and what that transition really looks like.

Client Convos: Emotional Investment Decisions

COVID produced one of the fastest market drops in modern history — and it gave me a tale of two clients I'll never forget.

The first came to me as a referral after the crash was already over. He had panicked during the downturn and sold everything, locking in a loss of over a million dollars. By the time he reached me, the market had already rebounded. There was nothing we could do to recover what he'd given away. He knew it. He told me plainly: he needed to get out of his own way. He couldn't be trusted to steward his own money through volatility. It was a hard and expensive lesson.

On the other side, I had retiree clients who felt every bit of that same fear. They called me. They were scared. And I said the same thing to all of them: trust the plan. Within a few months, everything had recovered. They called back — not scared this time, but grateful. Because they knew exactly what they would have done without that guidance. They'd watched it happen to someone else.

JUNE - MONTH 6

Pre-Retirement Planning

Transition, Not Just A Target

Retirement isn't a finish line—it's a transition. One of the biggest, most emotionally complex, and financially consequential transitions you'll ever make.

For years, retirement has likely lived in your head as a "someday" milestone. Maybe it was wrapped in visions of travel, rest, or simply freedom from the 9-to-5. But now, "someday" is getting closer—and it's time to move from abstract goals to actionable decisions.

June is about answering a powerful question:

What Are You Actually Retiring To?

Not just the dollars, but the days. Not just the savings, but the structure. Retirement planning isn't just about withdrawing from work. It's about stepping into a new season of purpose, rhythm, and confidence.

This Month, I'll Help You:

- Define what retirement looks like—financially and personally
- Understand how much is enough, and how to model for it
- Sort the needs from the wants (and everything in between)
- "Date" your retirement plan before committing fully

It's not just about readiness—it's about alignment. Because the most successful retirements aren't the richest ones. They're the ones that are most aligned with what matters.

WEEK 1

Are You Really Retirement Ready?

Income, Savings, And Mindset

Here's a surprising truth from two decades of advising clients: People often ask, "Can I afford to retire?" when the better question is "Am I ready to retire?"

That readiness has three dimensions:

1. **Financial:** Do you have enough to support the life you want?
2. **Logistical:** Do you have a clear plan for how money will flow?
3. **Emotional:** Do you know what you're retiring *to*, not just what you're leaving behind?

1. Financial Readiness

Most people focus here, and for good reason. Retirement shifts you from accumulation to decumulation. You're no longer saving—you're spending. And that shift can be disorienting.

Ask:

- What will my monthly expenses be—across needs, wants, and lifestyle?
- What income sources will I have (Social Security, pension, annuities)?
- Will my portfolio generate sustainable withdrawals?

If you haven't already modeled this out, now's the time. Even a simple projection (income vs. spending vs. asset drawdown) can be illuminating.

Tip: Many advisors recommend aiming to replace 70–80% of your pre-retirement income. But that's just a rule of thumb. Your actual number should reflect *your* life.

2. Logistical Readiness

You might have the savings. But do you know how to turn that into reliable income?

Start by identifying:

- Which accounts you'll draw from first (taxable vs. tax-deferred)
- How your taxes may change in retirement
- Whether your income will come monthly, quarterly, or "as needed"

A great plan removes guesswork. The more automated and predictable your income flows, the less anxiety you'll feel when the market wobbles or bills come due.

3. Emotional Readiness

This is the part people overlook—but it's often where the real work begins.

Ask yourself:

- How will I spend my time without work?
- Where will I find purpose, connection, or structure?
- Am I excited about this new chapter, or anxious about the unknown?

One client told me, "I didn't realize how much of my identity was tied to being needed at work. Retirement felt like drifting."

That's why we encourage clients to "test-drive" retirement—take extended time off, create a mock retirement schedule, even try living on your projected retirement budget for a few months. Don't just prepare your finances. Prepare your future life.

In my experience, 'Can I afford to retire?' is almost never the real question. The real question is: 'Will I still matter?' That one takes more than a spreadsheet to answer.

Action Step:

Schedule one hour this week to assess your readiness. Use these three buckets—**Financial, Logistical, Emotional**—and score yourself on a 1–10 scale in each. Where are you strongest? Where are the gaps? That's your roadmap for what comes next.

WEEK 2

Running Retirement Models

Turning Guesswork Into Strategy

Planning for retirement without a model is like planning a cross-country road trip without a map or GPS. You might make it, but you're relying on hope more than direction.

This week is about bringing clarity to that journey. By running retirement models, we can turn vague questions like "Will I have enough?" into actionable answers like "Here's what I need, when I need it, and how long it will last."

A model isn't about predicting the future. It's about preparing for a range of futures—and building confidence that your plan can weather them.

What A Retirement Model Actually Does

A retirement model is a financial projection that answers key questions:

- How much can I safely withdraw each year?
- When will my assets run out—or will they?
- What happens if inflation is higher than expected?
- How does retiring earlier (or later) affect my plan?
- How do taxes, investment returns, or Social Security decisions play into it?

You're stress-testing your future. And that's a good thing.

What Goes Into The Model

Here's what you (or your advisor) will need to input:

1. **Your retirement age**
    - Are you retiring all at once, or gradually phasing out?
2. **Expected expenses**
    - Needs (housing, food, healthcare)
    - Wants (travel, hobbies, gifting)
    - Surprises (repairs, medical events)
3. **Income sources**
    - Social Security (and when you'll claim it)
    - Pensions or annuities
    - Rental income or part-time work
4. **Portfolio value and allocation**
    - How much you've saved
    - How it's invested (stocks, bonds, cash)
    - Risk tolerance
5. **Assumptions**
    - Inflation (2–3% is typical)
    - Rate of return (based on your asset mix)
    - Tax treatment (ordinary income vs. capital gains)

Don't worry about making it perfect. Start with best estimates—you can always refine later.

What Makes A Good Retirement Model?

A good model balances **realism** with **flexibility**. It should:

- Be conservative enough to avoid false confidence
- Be flexible enough to update over time
- Include a **margin of safety** (a buffer for uncertainty)

Many planners run **Monte Carlo simulations**—a fancy term for stress-testing your plan through 1,000+ market scenarios, from best-case to worst-case. The output shows how often your plan "succeeds" under different conditions.

For example: If your plan has a 90% success rate, that means it held up in 900 out of 1,000 scenarios. That's peace of mind.

How Retirement Planning Tools Can Help

If you're working with an advisor, they likely use planning software like eMoney, RightCapital, or MoneyGuidePro. These tools bring the numbers to life with dynamic charts, timelines, and scenario testing.

If you're DIY-ing, tools like NewRetirement or Fidelity's retirement scorecard can provide a starting point. Even a spreadsheet can work—as long as it's updated regularly.

The #1 Rule: Revisit Often

Your retirement plan isn't a "set it and forget it" file. Life changes. Markets shift. Goals evolve.

The most successful retirees revisit their plan annually (or more often) to adjust:

- Spending patterns
- Tax strategies
- Investment allocation
- Healthcare or life expectancy changes

Think of your retirement model like a GPS: it only works if you update it when the road ahead changes.

Action Step:

Meet with your advisor—or use an online tool—to run your first retirement model. Focus on your core expenses, income sources, and safe withdrawal rate. Don't worry about perfection. The goal is progress, not precision.

WEEK 3

Sorting Needs, Wants, And Wishes

Prioritizing the Life You Want to Live

Retirement planning often begins with numbers. But behind those numbers are real lives—real days filled with routines, goals, relationships, and dreams.

That's why it's not just about *how much* you'll need in retirement, but *what you'll need it for.*

This week, we shift from spreadsheets to priorities—from assets to aspirations.

The Three Buckets: Needs, Wants, And Wishes

One of the most useful retirement frameworks breaks your expenses into three categories:

1. **Needs:** Your essential, non-negotiable living costs.

Think: Housing, food, healthcare, insurance, basic transportation, utilities. These are the expenses you must cover to maintain your lifestyle.

2. **Wants:** The comforts that enhance your life.

Travel, dining out, hobbies, entertainment, home upgrades, gifting. You could live without them, but they bring color and joy to retirement.

3. **Wishes:** The dreams that sit on your "someday" list.

A lake house. A round-the-world trip. Paying for your grandkids' college. These are aspirational—still possible, but not required for a fulfilling retirement.

This isn't just about budgeting. It's about defining *your* version of a meaningful life.

Why This Matters

Not all retirement plans fail because of poor investment returns. Many fall short because retirees haven't clearly prioritized.

When markets dip or unexpected expenses arise, clarity on needs vs. wants makes it easier to adapt without fear.

It also helps:

- Set more realistic withdrawal strategies
- Align investment risk to time horizon (e.g., funding needs with safer assets)
- Communicate clearly with your partner or advisor

And perhaps most importantly, having such clarity gives you permission to enjoy your money when the time comes.

How To Sort Your Expenses

You can do this on paper, in a spreadsheet, or during a planning session. Start by estimating what you plan to spend in retirement, and sort those numbers into three buckets.

Example (monthly):

- **Needs:**
    - Mortgage or rent: $2,000
    - Groceries: $600
    - Insurance: $400
    - Utilities: $300
    - Healthcare premiums: $500

Total Needs: $3,800

- **Wants:**
    - Travel: $800
    - Dining out: $300
    - Golf club: $200
    - Home improvement fund: $300

      Total Wants: $1,600
- **Wishes:**
    - Second home mortgage: $1,500
    - Charitable legacy fund: $500
    - Big international trip every 5 years: ~$500/ month average

      Total Wishes: $2,500

These numbers add up. And seeing them in categories helps clarify which expenses you could adjust if needed—without derailing your entire lifestyle.

Having The Conversation

If you're married or planning jointly, this exercise is especially valuable. You might be surprised at what your partner classifies as a "need" (golf?) or what you both agree could wait.

The goal isn't to judge—it's to align.

Bonus: Update Your Buckets Over Time

Your needs, wants, and wishes won't stay static.

- Early retirement might be more travel heavy.
- Later years might shift toward healthcare or legacy planning.
- Life events (like becoming a grandparent) could reshuffle your priorities.

Revisit these categories every few years or after major transitions. Your retirement plan should evolve with you.

Action Step:

Make a three-column list: Needs, Wants, Wishes. Assign a monthly (or annual) estimate to each. Then ask:

- Are your needs covered by stable income?
- Are your wants realistic based on your assets?
- Are your wishes on hold—or within reach?

This is how you build a retirement that's not just secure but deeply satisfying.

WEEK 4

Life Transitions In Retirement

I've started using a different word for this stage of life: rewirement. Not retirement — with all its connotations of stopping, stepping back, winding down. Rewirement. The idea that what you're doing isn't ending your productive life but reconnecting it to something that actually fits who you've become. The goal isn't less. It's truer.

Planning for the Phases of Your Next Chapter

Retirement isn't a finish line. It's a beginning, and like every new chapter, it comes with transitions.

Some are expected: slowing down, changing routines, living on a fixed income. Others are less predictable: health challenges, family changes, relocation, or even the emotional shift that may come with no longer "working."

This week is about preparing for those transitions—not just financially, but personally.

Because a good retirement plan isn't just about numbers. It's about navigating change with confidence.

Retirement Comes In Phases

Most people don't retire on a Friday and live the same way for the next 30 years. Retirement unfolds in stages, each with its own lifestyle, financial needs, and emotional shifts.

Here's a simplified framework:

Phase 1: The "Go-Go" Years (Early Retirement)

- Typically your 60s to early 70s
- High activity: travel, hobbies, volunteering, maybe even part-time work
- Health is relatively strong
- Spending often spikes early on (think: bucket list trips, second homes, big experiences)

Phase 2: The "Slow-Go" Years (Mid-Retirement)

- Usually your mid-70s to early 80s
- Pace slows, but you're still active
- Travel may decrease, but family time or local activities increase
- Medical expenses may begin to rise
- Spending starts to shift from wants to needs

Phase 3: The "No-Go" Years (Late Retirement)

- Often your mid-80s and beyond
- Focus turns to healthcare, housing, and end-of-life considerations
- Expenses may stabilize—or increase if long-term care becomes necessary
- Your plan needs to account for caregiving, estate execution, and support for your loved ones

Understanding these phases helps you plan for a retirement that's *realistic*, not idealized.

Emotional Transitions: Identity And Purpose

Many retirees underestimate the emotional shifts that accompany retirement.

Work often provides:

- Structure
- Social interaction
- A sense of purpose

When that's gone, it's common to feel disoriented, even if you're financially secure.

Key Questions To Consider:

- What will give me a sense of meaning in retirement?
- How will I structure my days?
- Who will I spend time with—and how?

Without intentionality, retirees can drift. With purpose, they thrive.

Financial Transitions To Prepare For

Here are some common shifts that can impact your plan:

- **Social Security Start Dates:** When will you claim? (It affects both your benefit and your spouse's.)
- **Medicare Enrollment:** At 65, healthcare becomes a major factor—mistakes here can be costly.
- **Required Minimum Distributions (RMDs):** These usually begin at age 73 and can impact your taxes significantly. It's important to note the RMD age isn't always 73, so it's best to talk to an advisor about this.
- **Changing Housing Needs:** Will you downsize? Relocate? Consider aging-in-place upgrades?
- **Legacy and Gifting:** Do you plan to help your kids/grandkids during your lifetime?

Each of these transitions should be considered in your plan—not reacted to when they happen.

Flexibility Is A Superpower

Retirement doesn't reward perfection. It rewards adaptability. That's why your plan should include:

- A healthy cash reserve
- Flexible withdrawal strategies (e.g., guardrails or dynamic spending)
- Room for joy—and room for surprises

The goal isn't to predict every turn. It's to be ready to adjust when life changes.

Don't Navigate This Alone

This stage of life is too important—and too complex—to go it alone.

A good advisor does more than run numbers. They help you think through:

- Lifestyle design
- Tax planning over decades, not just for one year
- Healthcare coverage and long-term care planning
- How your legacy aligns with your values

You're not just planning for retirement. You're planning for how you want to live—and how you want to be remembered.

Action Step:

Sketch out your vision of each phase:

- What does your ideal "Go-Go" period look like?
- What support might you need in the "Slow-Go" or "No-Go" years?

- Are there any transitions you haven't yet planned for, like downsizing, caregiving, or shifting your purpose?

This is your next chapter. Make it one you look forward to.

Wrapping Up June

Retirement is closer than it feels — and more complex than just a number. You've started thinking about what you're retiring to, not just what you're leaving behind. That distinction matters more than most people realize.

Next month, we get into the mechanics — how to turn everything you've saved into a reliable, lasting income stream.

Client Convos: Retirement Readiness

A client came in at 65 years old convinced he wasn't ready to retire. He had a number in his head — a magic number — and he was certain he hadn't reached it yet. He was prepared to work another five years.

We went through everything together: his expenses, his lifestyle, his goals, what retirement actually looked like for him day to day. And when the plan was built, the math was clear: he could retire right now.

He didn't believe me. He asked me to run it again. Then again. Ten different times, in different ways, we walked through the same analysis. And every time, it came back the same. He didn't need five more years. He retired five months after we met. Not because he got lucky — because he finally had a plan built around his actual life, not around a number he'd invented in his head.

JULY - MONTH 7

Retirement Income Planning

Turning Your Savings Into A Paycheck That Lasts

You've worked for decades, saved consistently, and watched your accounts grow. But now comes the big question: How do you turn that pile of savings into a reliable, lasting income?

This month is all about **retirement income strategy**: making sure the money you've accumulated doesn't just sit there, but actively supports your life.

Because retirement isn't just about what you *have*. It's about what you can *use*—when, and how sustainably.

This is where accumulation becomes decumulation. And it requires a very different mindset.

You'll Learn:

- How to build a retirement "paycheck" from various income sources
- Why sequence of returns matters more than average returns

- How to choose the right withdrawal strategy for your situation
- Why taxes and timing can make or break your income plan
- How to build guardrails so you don't run out—or shortchange yourself

Let's turn your nest egg into a plan.

WEEK 1

The Retirement Paycheck—Where Income Comes From Now

Once you stop working, your financial life changes.

No more biweekly paychecks. No more employer benefits. But the bills? They still show up.

So the first step in retirement income planning is understanding **where your money will come from now**—and how to organize those sources into a steady, dependable stream.

Your Retirement Income Bucket List

Here are the most common sources of income in retirement:

1. **Social Security**

o Often forms the foundation of retirement income.

o Claiming age impacts the size of your benefit (62 vs. 67 vs. 70).

o Spousal, survivor, and delayed retirement credits add complexity.

2. **Pensions (if applicable)**

o Less common today, but still relevant for government, military, and some private sector employees.

o You may need to choose between lump sum or monthly payments, as well as single or joint survivor benefits.

3. **Investment Accounts**

o 401(k), 403(b), IRA, Roth IRA, brokerage accounts.

o These become your private paychecks—but withdrawing requires planning.

o Tax treatment varies by account type (taxable, tax-deferred, or tax-free).

4. **Annuities or Income Products**

o Some retirees use annuities to create guaranteed lifetime income

o Not for everyone, but useful in certain situations.

5. **Part-Time Work or Consulting**

o Some choose to continue working at a reduced capacity

o Provides income and structure or purpose.

6. **Rental Income or Passive Income Streams**

o From real estate, royalties, or small business stakes.

7. **Required Minimum Distributions (RMDs)**

o Usually starting at age 73 (but this can change so check with current guidelines), the government requires withdrawals from traditional IRAs and 401(k)s.

The Coordination Challenge

Each of these sources has different rules, risks, and tax consequences.

The goal is not just to know what you have, but to **coordinate them strategically**.

That means:

- Timing your Social Security to maximize benefits

- Deciding when and how to draw from your investment accounts
- Minimizing taxes across accounts
- Keeping enough liquidity for short-term needs
- Ensuring income lasts as long as you do

The Retirement Paycheck Framework

Here's a simple but powerful way to think about structuring your income:

Rather than trying to match specific expenses to specific income sources — which works in theory but rarely in practice — think of your portfolio as a single, coordinated pool that funds your life.

An approach we use with clients called spend-and-replenish works like this: you draw what you need each month from a cash reserve (typically enough years of expenses held in cash or short-term bonds to hold you through any downturn or worries), and then periodically replenish that reserve from your longer-term investments. This keeps you from having to sell growth assets at the wrong time — during a market dip, for example — while still making sure your money continues working for you.

A common starting point is withdrawing 4–5% of your portfolio annually, adjusted over time based on market performance and your spending needs. The key word is adjusted — this isn't a fixed number you set and forget - it's a framework you revisit.

The most important principle: don't go all cash in retirement. It feels safe, but inflation quietly erodes purchasing power over a 20–30 year retirement. You still need growth. The goal is to balance liquidity for near-term needs with growth for the long term — not to eliminate risk entirely, but to manage it thoughtfully.

Avoiding The Big Mistake: Going Ad Hoc

Many retirees start by just pulling money when they need it. No strategy. No sustainability.

That's how accounts get drained too fast—or taxes get out of hand.

Instead, treat retirement income like you treated your paycheck years ago: it should be **planned**, **predictable**, and **purposeful.**

I've watched two clients with nearly identical portfolios arrive at retirement and have wildly different experiences — not because of the market, but because of the plan. One had a strategy, a sequence, a monthly number they could count on. The other figured it out as they went. One slept at night. The other called me every time the Dow moved.

Action Step:

List all your potential income sources in retirement. Then categorize them as either:

- **Guaranteed** (e.g., Social Security, pension, annuity)
- **Variable** (e.g., investment withdrawals, rental income)

Estimate how much you expect from each, and start thinking about how to match those dollars to your expenses.

WEEK 2

Withdrawal Strategies That Work

How to Take Money Out Without Running Out

You've spent decades learning how to **save and invest**. Now it's time to learn how to **withdraw and preserve**.

This is where many retirees get it wrong—not because they're careless, but because withdrawing money is deceptively complex.

Take too little, and you might shortchange your lifestyle. Take too much, too soon—or from the wrong account—and you risk running out early, triggering tax headaches, or leaving less than you intended.

This week is about how to draw down your assets **intentionally, sustainably**, and **strategically.**

The Retirement Math Problem

Here's the challenge: Your retirement could last **25–35+ years.** Your portfolio needs to last just as long—maybe longer.

You're not just living off your savings. You're asking those savings to *keep growing* while also *supporting your lifestyle.*

That requires balance. It also requires a plan.

Key Withdrawal Strategies

Let's look at a few of the most common—and most effective—methods:

1. The 4% Rule (Starting Point, Not Gospel)

- Based on historical data, withdrawing **4% of your portfolio in the first year** and adjusting for inflation annually *might* provide 30+ years of income.
- Example: $1 million portfolio → $40,000 first-year withdrawal
- Caution: This rule doesn't account for market volatility, taxes, or personal goals. It's a guideline, not a guarantee.

2. Guardrail Strategy (Dynamic Spending)

- Start with a set withdrawal rate (e.g., 4%), but adjust based on portfolio performance.
    - If markets soar, you can increase withdrawals.
    - If markets drop, you reduce spending temporarily.
- It offers flexibility and helps extend portfolio longevity.
-

3. Bucket Strategy (Time Segmentation)

- Divide your assets into three "buckets" based on when you'll need the money:
    1. **Short-Term (0–2 years):** Cash or cash equivalents
    2. **Mid-Term (2–10 years):** Bonds, CDs, conservative investments
    3. **Long-Term (10+ years):** Stocks and growth assets
- It helps you manage risk, stay invested, and avoid selling stocks during downturns.

Additional Considerations:

• **Required Minimum Distributions (RMDs)**
o Starting at age 73 (generally, but check current guidelines), the IRS requires you to take distributions from traditional IRAs, 401(k)s, and similar accounts.
o Failing to take your RMDs can trigger a 25% penalty—a costly mistake.
o Plan ahead to avoid a tax hit or forced liquidation.
• **Roth Conversions (Strategic, Not Automatic)**
o Moving funds from a traditional IRA to a Roth IRA lets you pay taxes now, then enjoy tax-free growth and withdrawals later.
o Done over time and in low-tax years, this can be a powerful planning tool.
o It's especially helpful before RMDs begin or if you expect higher tax rates in the future.

Withdrawal Sequence Matters

The **order** in which you withdraw from different account types can significantly affect your tax bill and portfolio longevity.

A common sequence:

1. **Taxable accounts** (brokerage): Use capital gains first
2. **Tax-deferred accounts** (Traditional IRA/401(k)): Withdraw strategically based on RMDs and tax brackets
3. **Tax-free accounts** (Roth IRA): Let grow as long as possible for future flexibility

But this isn't one-size-fits-all. Your ideal sequence depends on:

- Your tax bracket
- Other income (Social Security, pensions)

- Healthcare costs
- Legacy goals

The Hidden Risk: Sequence Of Returns

If the market drops early in your retirement—and you're withdrawing during that dip—your portfolio may not recover.

This is called **sequence risk**, and it's one of the biggest threats to retirement success.

Two retirees with the same average return can have **wildly different outcomes** based on the *timing* of those returns.

That's why withdrawal flexibility and cash reserves matter.

Behavioral Bias To Watch: The Sunk Cost Fallacy

You may feel attached to a certain stock, fund, or investment because it's "done well for years."

But holding on out of nostalgia or fear of regret—when it no longer serves your needs—can sabotage your withdrawal plan.

Retirement income planning is not about past performance. It's about future utility.

Action Step:

Estimate your essential monthly expenses in retirement. Then identify which income sources or withdrawals will cover them. Run a basic simulation or speak to your advisor about different withdrawal strategies—and how long your current portfolio might last under each.

WEEK 3

Taxes, Timing & Maximizing What You Keep

Why Retirement Income Isn't Just About How Much You Withdraw—But How

Most people think retirement income planning is about figuring out **how much they can spend.**
But just as important—and often overlooked—is **how much of that money you actually keep** after taxes.

In retirement, *you* control more of your tax outcome than ever before. There's no paycheck withholding. You decide which accounts to pull from, how much to take, and when to take it.

That means smart planning can help you stretch your income —and your legacy—farther.

The Retirement Tax Landscape

In retirement, your income might come from a variety of sources:

- Social Security
- Traditional IRAs and 401(k)s
- Roth IRAs
- Taxable investment accounts
- Pensions or annuities
- Part-time work or consulting

Each of these sources may be taxed differently. The mix you choose matters—a lot.

Common Tax Pitfalls To Avoid

1. Required Minimum Distribution Shock

Starting at age 73 (although RMD requirements often change, so check with the IRS and your advisor), Required Minimum Distributions (RMDs) can push you into a higher tax bracket—just when you thought your taxes would go down.

Solution: Start strategizing in your 60s. Consider making partial Roth conversions or drawing from IRAs earlier.

2. Social Security Taxation Surprise

Many retirees are surprised to learn that up to **85% of their Social Security benefits may be taxable,** depending on their income. This is determined using a formula called provisional income, which includes other retirement income sources, tax-free interest, and part of your Social Security benefits. Your full retirement age may impact this, so consult with an advisor.

Solution: Plan withdrawals strategically across different account types. In some cases, delaying Social Security can increase your benefit and create opportunities for more tax-efficient planning earlier in retirement.

3. Capital Gains Missteps

Selling appreciated assets at the wrong time can trigger higher taxes—and even impact your Medicare premiums.

Solution: Use tax-loss harvesting, time sales in lower-income years, or gift appreciated assets to charity.

Key Strategies To Maximize What You Keep

1. Roth Conversions (Again—Because They Matter)

Move money from tax-deferred accounts (like traditional IRAs) into tax-free Roth accounts while you're in a low bracket.

This reduces future RMDs and creates more tax-free income options later.

2. Tax Bracket Management

Be proactive: Fill up your lower tax brackets with intentional withdrawals or conversions. For example:

- If your marginal bracket is 12%, consider converting IRA dollars to a Roth *up to the top of that bracket.*
- Doing this over several years can help reduce your total lifetime tax burden.

3. Qualified Charitable Distributions

Once you turn 70 ½, you can give directly from your IRA to a qualified charity—**and reduce your taxable income** in the process.

This is a win-win for retirees who are charitably inclined.

4. Asset Location (Not Just Allocation)

It's not just *what* you invest in; it's *where* you hold it.

- **Tax-deferred accounts:** Hold income-generating investments (bonds, REITs)
- **Roth accounts:** Prioritize high-growth investments (stocks)
- **Taxable accounts:** Focus on tax-efficient investments

(ETFs, muni bonds)

This approach helps reduce taxes on dividends and gains—and increases what you get to keep.

A Word On Medicare And Income Related Monthly Adjustment Amount

Your income doesn't just affect your taxes; it can also increase your Medicare premiums.

Higher income = **higher premiums** under the Income-Related Monthly Adjustment Amount (IRMAA).

Smart tax planning can help you stay below key thresholds and avoid surprises.

Behavioral Bias To Watch: Anchoring

Many retirees assume their retirement taxes will always be lower. They "anchor" to their working income tax rates and underestimate how RMDs, Social Security, and portfolio withdrawals interact.

Anchoring on assumptions—rather than projections—can lead to underplanning and overpaying.

Action Step:

Review your projected income sources and tax brackets for the next 5–10 years. Ask your advisor or tax professional:

- Are there opportunities to convert, withdraw, or donate strategically?
- How can I structure my income to stay in the most favorable tax zone?

A little planning now can preserve thousands—maybe even

hundreds of thousands—over time.

WEEK 4

From Income To Impact—Designing Your Retirement Lifestyle

Why Retirement Is About More Than Money

What you've known about investing in retirement is about to get flipped on its head. Instead of maximizing your risk-adjusted return, it's now about investing to **maximize your lifestyle** in retirement. The rules, mindset, and strategies are different.

You've spent a career earning, saving, and planning. Retirement is the chapter where those efforts pay off—not just in dollars, but in *choices*.

This week is about moving from **survival mode** to **intentional living**. It's about using your income to create a lifestyle you're proud of, one that reflects your values, priorities, and impact.

Retirement Isn't An Ending—It's A Reallocation

- Time becomes your most valuable asset.
- Your calendar becomes a blank slate.
- Your spending becomes a reflection of your values.

So the key question becomes: **"What do I want my life to look like now?"**

Redefining Wealth In Retirement

It's not just about how much you have. It's about how your money helps you:

- Spend time with the people you love

- Support the causes you care about
- Take care of your health and happiness
- Leave a legacy—not just financially, but emotionally and relationally

Create A Values-Based Spending Plan

In retirement, your income may feel "fixed," but your priorities don't have to be.

Step 1: Name Your Top Three Retirement Priorities.

Examples:

- Family and grandchildren
- Travel or seasonal living
- Health and wellness
- Hobbies, passion projects, or volunteer work
- Charities or community involvement

Step 2: Audit Your Budget To Reflect Those Priorities.

Ask: *Does my spending match what matters most to me?*

You may find it's time to shift money away from habits and toward purpose.

The Joy Factor: Guilt-Free Spending In Retirement

Many retirees feel **hesitant** to enjoy their money—worried about running out, about markets, about "spending too soon."

But the point of good planning is to create permission.

Permission to spend.

Permission to enjoy.

Permission to say yes.

When your income plan is solid and your needs are met, it's okay to *let go of guilt.*

You've earned this.

Planning For Impact, Not Just Income

Retirement also creates new opportunities for **giving**—of time, energy, and money.

Ask yourself:

- What do I want to be remembered for?
- Are there people or causes I want to support while I'm alive, not just in a will?
- Is there wisdom or experience I want to pass down?

This is where your legacy starts: not with a number, but with intention.

Designing Your Retirement Lifestyle

Instead of drifting, take time to design:

- What your ideal day, week, or month looks like
- Where you want to live and *how* you want to live there
- What routines or commitments bring meaning and joy
- How much structure vs. spontaneity you want

A great retirement isn't built by default—it's created on purpose.

Behavioral Bias To Watch: Lifestyle Creep

Even in retirement, it's easy for spending to slowly expand. You upgrade, indulge, or get used to a higher lifestyle, and suddenly the math starts to tighten.

Regular check-ins can help ensure your spending stays aligned with your long-term goals.

Action Step:

Write down your top three values for this stage of life. Then ask:

- *How does my spending reflect these values?*
- *What might I want to do more of—and what can I release?*

If retirement is the reward for decades of work, make sure you're actually enjoying the reward.

◆◆◆

Wrapping Up July

Turning savings into income is a different skill than building it — and now you have a framework for doing it intentionally. A plan, a sequence, and a strategy for staying flexible will serve you far better than figuring it out as you go.

Next month, we zoom in on one of the most emotionally charged financial decisions families face — planning for college without sacrificing your own future.

Client Convos: Withdrawal In Retirement

A client came to me who had done everything right on the accumulation side. Decades of disciplined, aggressive investing. He had built real wealth — and he was proud of it, rightfully so.

Then he retired. And he quickly discovered that the skills and instincts that built the portfolio had almost nothing to do with protecting and distributing it. He had no income drawdown strategy. He had no sequence-of-returns plan. He was improvising — and a bad stretch of markets early in retirement can be devastating in a way that a bad stretch during accumulation simply isn't.

He hired us. We built a customized income strategy. And the shift in him was remarkable. The client who had been hyper-engaged in every market movement — checking accounts daily, always with an opinion — became someone who trusted the process. He went from managing his money to living his life. That's the transition retirement planning is actually supposed to create.

AUGUST - MONTH 8

College Planning & Education

I'm writing this chapter not just as an advisor, but as a dad with three kids who will, one day, be doing exactly what the families in this chapter are navigating. That gives me a different kind of investment in getting this right.

You can borrow for school—but not for retirement.

Few topics blend emotional intensity and financial complexity quite like college planning. It's one of the few times in your financial life when your heart and your wallet might be pointed in completely different directions. We want to give our children or grandchildren every opportunity. We want to open doors, expand horizons, and provide the kind of life we worked hard to build.

But here's the challenge: College is one of the most expensive line items in many families' financial plans—and it comes right as retirement planning is shifting into high gear.

So, how do you provide for your children's education without sacrificing your own financial security?

That's the question we'll tackle this month. Too often, people delay saving for retirement so they can fund education. But while your child can take out loans for school, you can't borrow for your retirement. That's why smart education planning is not just about *how much* you save, but *how*, *when*, and *why*.

We'll cover the most common—and misunderstood—college funding tools, talk about the emotional pressure behind education decisions, and help you separate what's truly valuable from what's just expensive. Whether you're saving for a newborn or helping a grandchild finish their degree, this month is about building a plan rooted in *values*, *clarity*, and *balance*.

Key Topics:

- Choosing between 529s, custodial accounts, and other vehicles
- Scholarship strategy and why it matters early
- Realistic expectations about school pricing and ROI
- Multi-generational planning opportunities
- Aligning education with your family's core values

You don't need to overpay to do what's right for your family. But you do need to plan ahead.

WEEK 1

College Savings Vehicles—529s, Custodial Accounts, & Grandparent Strategies

When people start thinking about saving for college, the first reaction is usually either panic or avoidance. With tuition rising faster than inflation and sticker prices now pushing $80,000 a year at some private universities, many parents feel paralyzed before they even start.

But here's the truth: You don't have to save the full cost of college by the time your child turns 18. You just need a plan. And the sooner you start, the more options—and flexibility—you'll have.

529 Plans: The Most Valuable Player Of Education Savings

A 529 college savings plan remains one of the most powerful tools for education funding.

Why it works:

- **Tax-deferred growth** and **tax-free withdrawals** for qualified education expenses
- **High contribution limits**, often over $300,000 per beneficiary, depending on the state
- **State tax benefits** in many states for residents who contribute to their in-state plan
- **Broad usage**—can be used for college, some K–12 tuition, apprenticeships, and even student loan repayment (up to $10,000)

But recent legislation has made 529s even more attractive.

New Flexibility: 529s To Roth Individual Retirement Accounts

Starting in 2024, unused funds in a 529 plan can be rolled into a Roth IRA for the beneficiary—up to $35,000 over a lifetime, assuming certain conditions are met. This helps eliminate the fear of "What if my kid doesn't go to college?" or "What if we overfund it?"

Custodial Accounts (Uniform Gifts To Minors Act Or Uniform Transfers To Minors Act): More Freedom, More Risk

Custodial accounts offer flexibility: funds can be used for *anything* that benefits the child, not just education. But that flexibility comes with trade-offs:

- **Less favorable tax treatment** than 529s
- **Counts as the student's asset**, which can reduce financial aid eligibility
- **No strings attached** once the child reaches the age of majority (18 or 21, depending on the state)

In short, if your child might not be financially mature at 18, think twice before overfunding a custodial account.

Grandparents & Multi-Generational Planning

For many families, grandparents want to help but don't want to overstep. A grandparent-owned 529 used to be a financial aid landmine. Distributions were counted as student income, which could dramatically reduce aid eligibility.

That's now changed.

As of the 2024–2025 school year, the new simplified FAFSA no longer counts grandparent 529 distributions as income for the student. That opens the door for multi-generational wealth planning:

- Grandparents can fund education **without hurting aid eligibility**.
- Parents can prioritize retirement while grandparents support college savings.
- Families can coordinate to avoid overfunding one account.

This change also raises the importance of *ownership structure* —the individual who owns the 529 may impact not just taxes but planning flexibility.

Planning Tip: Don't Overthink Perfection

Too many people get stuck comparing plan performance, state tax benefits, or investment choices—and never actually open the account. It's more important to get started than to get it perfect. You can always adjust later.

Action Step:

If you haven't opened a 529 plan, now's the time. If you have one, review it. Are the contributions aligned with your savings goals? Have you designated a successor owner? If you're a grandparent, consider whether you want to open your own 529 or contribute to an existing one.

Key Questions:

- Who owns the account?
- What's your savings target?

- How will you coordinate savings between parents and grandparents?
- Are you taking advantage of any state tax incentives?

WEEK 2

Scholarships & Realistic Expectations

When it comes to college funding, families often assume scholarships will be the great equalizer, helping close the gap between tuition and what they can afford. But here's what most people don't realize: Scholarships are not a one-size-fits-all solution, and they're rarely the golden ticket people hope for.

This week, we're going to reset expectations around scholarships—and show you how to make the most of what's actually available.

The Myth Of The Full Ride

Hollywood loves a good "full ride" story. But in real life, full-ride scholarships are exceedingly rare, especially at elite schools. According to the National Center for Education Statistics, fewer than **1% of students** receive enough scholarships and grants to cover the full cost of college.

Instead, most scholarships cover **small pieces** of the puzzle: $500 here, $1,000 there. Valuable? Absolutely. But expecting a full ride can create a false sense of security and lead to under-saving.

Merit Vs. Need-Based Aid

There are two main types of scholarships and financial aid:

- **Merit-based aid:** awarded for academic, athletic, or artistic achievement
- **Need-based aid:** based on your family's financial circumstances

Here's the twist: most top-tier schools have enormous endowments and offer **generous need-based aid**, but very few offer merit-based scholarships. Meanwhile, less competitive schools may offer **substantial merit aid** to attract strong students.

Understanding where your child is likely to shine can help you focus your application strategy. Sometimes the "best" school isn't the most expensive—it's the one offering the best package.

Start Early—And Stay Organized

Scholarship applications often require essays, transcripts, recommendations, and time. The earlier you start, the better your chances. Encourage your child to treat scholarships like a part-time job in their junior and senior years of high school.

There are also thousands of **private scholarships** available, many with very specific eligibility (e.g., community service, parent's employer, ethnic background, intended major). They often fly under the radar, but small awards add up.

Pro Tip: Set a goal of applying to **one scholarship a week** during application season.

Realistic Expectations Lead To Smarter Planning

Instead of banking on scholarships to solve everything, use them to **supplement** a broader education funding strategy. That includes:

- Saving in a 529 or other vehicle
- Having open conversations with your student about cost, school choice, and what's financially realistic
- Comparing **net price** (after aid and scholarships), not just sticker price

The Return On Investment Of A Degree Matters

One of the most important but overlooked parts of education planning is understanding **what you're paying for**. Is the degree likely to generate a return on investment?

In other words:

- Will the career your child is pursuing support their student loan burden?
- Are there alternatives—like starting at a community college or in-state school—that offer similar outcomes at lower cost?

We're not saying money should drive every decision. But ignoring the financial side entirely can saddle your child with debt they'll be paying off for decades.

Action Step:

Sit down with your student and map out the schools they're considering. Research:

- Each school's **average aid package**
- Whether they offer **merit aid** (many top schools do not)
- Total **cost of attendance** vs. your savings and expected contribution

Have an honest discussion about what is and isn't financially feasible. This isn't just about saying "no" to expensive schools—it's about saying "yes" to financial freedom down the road.

WEEK 3

Aligning Education With Your Values

Choosing a college—or any post-secondary path—is one of the most consequential financial decisions a family makes. Yet so often, it's driven by emotion, brand name, or outdated assumptions about "success." This week, we're pausing to ask a deeper question:

Does your education plan reflect your family's values?

Because how we spend money is often the clearest reflection of what we believe.

Step Back From The Prestige Game

It's easy to get swept into the prestige race. Maybe you've had your eye on a dream school, a legacy school, or a school with a name that makes friends and neighbors nod in approval. But here's the thing: an institution's sticker price does not determine your child's future.

Success in life is shaped far more by **work ethic**, **relationships**, and **adaptability** than by the pedigree of a person's degree.

So before you lock in an application list—or co-sign a mountain of student debt—ask:

- What matters most to us as a family?
- What do we hope this experience will teach our child beyond academics?
- Are we choosing this school because it aligns with our goals ... or because it impresses other people?

Know What You're Paying For

College is not just about getting a degree—it's about launching a young adult into independence. So ask yourself: Does this school offer more than just a brand name?

Think about:

- **Career readiness:** Does it provide internships, job placement, and alumni networking?
- **Student support:** Are there resources for mental health, tutoring, and mentorship?
- **Return on investment:** What's the average starting salary for graduates in your child's intended major?

You are not just funding four years; you're investing in a lifetime of impact. Make sure the value aligns with the cost.

There's More Than One Path To Success

College isn't the only route to a fulfilling, financially stable life. And the "best" path isn't the same for every student.

Consider:

- **Community college and transfer pathways**
- **Apprenticeships and trade programs**
- **Gap years with work, service, or travel**
- **Military service with education benefits**

These options may not be flashy, but for some students, they're a better match—and a far smarter financial decision.

Encourage your child to explore who they are and how they learn best. Education isn't just about the next four years. It's about building a foundation for the decades that follow.

Let Values Lead

Every family's values are different. Maybe your priority is avoiding debt. Maybe it's faith-based education, or staying close to home, or ensuring your child enters adulthood without a financial burden you carry into retirement.

Whatever your values are, **define them clearly** and **let them guide your decisions.**

Don't be afraid to say no to a "dream school" if it doesn't match your long-term financial vision. Helping your child graduate with a solid start—and a strong sense of values—is more important than a fancy diploma.

Here's what I tell clients — and what I'll tell my own kids: The name on the diploma matters far less than what you do with the four years you spend earning it. I've watched graduates from state schools outwork and outlast graduates from brand-name institutions their whole careers. Curiosity and work ethic aren't taught by prestige.

Action Step:

As a family, take time this week to complete a "college values checklist." Sit down with your student and talk about:

- What matters most in their college experience?
- What's negotiable—and what's not?
- How will your family's financial values shape the decision?

The goal isn't to eliminate emotion from the process but to ensure your decisions are rooted in something deeper than rankings.

WEEK 4

Balancing Family Goals With Financial Reality

You want the best for your child. Every parent does. But when it comes to education, the best choice isn't always the most expensive one. This week, we're going to talk about how to balance **your family's dreams for your children** with the **financial reality** you're navigating today—and what you'll need for the future.

Because college planning isn't just about your child's goals. It's also about protecting yours.

The Real Cost Of "Just One More Year"

Let's say you're 52 and hoping to retire at 65. You still have a mortgage, you're helping your parents, and you'd love to spend more time traveling. But now you're facing a $40,000/year tuition bill—times four years, per child.

That's $160,000 per kid. And if you have two or three kids?

That number can hit **half a million dollars**.

Ask yourself:

- Can we comfortably pay this without derailing our retirement savings?
- Are we taking on debt that could follow us—or our child—for decades?
- If we delay our own goals, what's the long-term tradeoff?

You're not failing your child if you set boundaries. You're modeling financial wisdom and teaching them how to live within limits.

Your Retirement Still Matters

Here's the thing: **There are loans for college—but there are no loans for retirement.**

If you spend everything now on tuition, you may end up dependent on your child later. That's not a gift to them. It's a burden.

It's okay to say:

"We can contribute X amount toward your education. Beyond that, we'll need to explore scholarships, work-study, or other funding."

That conversation might feel hard. But it's also honest, empowering, and respectful of your child's growing independence.

Avoid The Guilt Trap

Many parents feel torn between financial responsibility and emotional obligation. Maybe you didn't go to college, and you want your child to have what you didn't. Or maybe your parents paid for your school, and you feel you "owe it" to do the same.

But here's a truth that's often unspoken:

Sacrificing your financial security doesn't guarantee their success.

Your kids need more than your money. They need your example. Teaching them about financial boundaries can become one of the most important lessons you pass down.

Create A Plan Together

Instead of making education decisions in isolation, make your child a partner in the process. Talk to them about:

- The total cost of attendance
- What your family can contribute
- What student loan debt would mean for their future
- The difference in ROI between schools and degrees

Use this as an opportunity to teach them about budgeting, long-term planning, and how to weigh trade-offs. This is one of their first big adult decisions—guide them through it.

Action Step:

This week, run the numbers. Look at your current financial plan and ask:

- How much can we reasonably contribute to education?
- What are we willing to sacrifice—and what are we not?
- How does this fit with our broader goals like retirement, travel, or giving?

Then set a family meeting to review everything together. Create a plan that's not just based on dreams, but one that's sustainable, realistic, and values-aligned.

◆ ◆ ◆

Wrapping Up August

Education planning is really values planning. By separating emotion from strategy — and protecting your retirement in the process — you've given your family something more valuable than a tuition check: a clear-eyed plan.

Next month, we step back from the numbers entirely — looking at the emotional side of money, and why understanding your relationship with it may be the most important planning work you do.

Client Convos: College Planning

I have this conversation constantly. Parents come in and tell me they're going to pay for their kids' college. Full stop. Non-negotiable. And I respect that. But I always ask the follow-up question: have you seen what that actually costs, and do you know what it means for everything else?

I had clients with three kids who had made this commitment without really running the numbers. When we modeled it out — tuition, room and board, four years each, at the schools they had in mind — it was approaching a million dollars. And when we showed them what that capital would otherwise produce over the same time horizon, and what it meant for their own retirement timeline, it reframed the entire conversation.

They didn't abandon the goal. They recalibrated it. They decided to contribute meaningfully — but not unconditionally. They protected their own retirement track while still supporting their kids within reason. The point was never to talk them out of generosity. It was to make sure the generosity was intentional, not reflexive.

SEPTEMBER - MONTH 9

Your Relationship with Money

Money is never just about numbers.

It may show up in spreadsheets, budgets, and portfolios, but its roots run deeper. Behind every financial decision is a story: how you grew up, what you believe is possible, what you fear, and what you value most.

This month is about something we don't often talk about in financial planning: the emotional side of money.

Most financial education focuses on "what to do"—save more, spend less, invest wisely. But very rarely are we asked to think about *why* we do what we do. Why we feel anxious checking our bank accounts. Why we overextend to help others or can't seem to enjoy spending, even when we can afford it. Why some people tie their self-worth to their net worth, while others avoid discussing money altogether.

Those patterns aren't random. They're learned. Inherited. Reinforced.

And until we confront them, they quietly run the show.

This month is about slowing down and stepping back, taking a deeper look at your relationship with money and how it's shaping your life. It's about replacing shame with self-awareness and judgment with curiosity. Because money doesn't just support your lifestyle—it reveals it. And sometimes, it restricts it.

We'll Explore:

- Where your beliefs about money began and whether they still serve you
- The hidden emotions that drive your spending and saving behaviors
- What happens when couples bring different money stories into one household
- How to rewrite the narratives that no longer fit the life you're building

Your financial life isn't just a series of transactions. It's a reflection of your identity, values, habits, and history. By understanding the forces behind your decisions, you gain the power to reshape your path forward—not just financially, but emotionally.

This month isn't about adding a new tool to your money toolkit. It's about stepping into a new level of clarity—one where your money no longer controls your story, but supports it.

WEEK 1

What Really Makes People Happy?

Let's start with a simple but revealing question:

What would you do if you suddenly received $1 million, no strings attached?

Most people have an answer ready—pay off debt, buy a home, take a dream vacation, maybe retire early. These answers are perfectly valid. But they also reflect something deeper: we believe that money is the key to happiness. And in some ways, that's true. But not in the way we often assume.

We live in a world that's constantly selling us the idea that "more" is the solution—more income, more square footage, more luxury, more status. Yet study after study confirms something that might surprise you: Once your basic needs are met, more money doesn't necessarily translate to more happiness.

So what does?

The Money-Happiness Tipping Point

Research has shown that **happiness increases with income, but only up to a certain point.** That point, depending on where you live and what your circumstances are, usually hovers around the amount needed to meet your essential expenses and reduce financial stress. Beyond that, the marginal benefit of each additional dollar quickly drops off.

Once survival and stability are taken care of, the question becomes:

How are you using your money?

It turns out, it's not the amount of money that makes us happy; it's how we manage it, spend it, and align it with our values. Let's break down the three key factors most often associated with real financial well-being and happiness:

1. Autonomy And Control

When people say they want more money, what they often mean is:

"I want more control over my life."

Money gives you choices. It gives you the ability to say no to things that don't align with your values and yes to the things that do. It allows you to leave a toxic job, move to a city you love, take time off to care for your health or family, or start a business you believe in.

Financial freedom isn't necessarily about being rich—it's about having enough control over your money that you can live on your own terms.

Ask yourself:

Where does money give me freedom?

Where does it still feel like a source of pressure or a limitation?

2. Experiences Over Things

You've probably heard the phrase: "Spend on experiences, not stuff." And there's good reason for that. Psychologists have found that we tend to derive **more lasting happiness from experiences**—traveling, spending time with loved ones, learning something new—than from material possessions.

Why?

- **Experiences get better in memory:** A family trip may have had hiccups in the moment, but over time, those stories become the things you cherish.
- **Experiences strengthen relationships:** Sharing time

and connection with others creates deeper bonds.

- **Stuff depreciates, memories appreciate:** That new gadget loses its sparkle quickly. But an experience stays with you, and often grows more valuable over time.

If your goal is to maximize joy per dollar, start looking at your budget through this lens. The return on investment for a memorable experience often beats anything you could buy at the store.

3. Giving As A Happiness Strategy

This might be the most counterintuitive truth of all:

Generosity makes people happier.

People who give—through charitable donations, supporting friends and family, or even volunteering their time—report higher levels of life satisfaction. Giving activates the reward centers of our brain and connects us to a deeper sense of purpose and community.

The amount doesn't have to be large. What matters is the **act of contribution**, of moving beyond yourself and creating value for someone else. It shifts the mindset from scarcity to abundance and reinforces the idea that you have enough to share.

If you've never thought about giving as part of your financial strategy, now might be the time to start. It doesn't have to be formal or flashy, just intentional.

Reframing Success

So often, we measure financial success in terms of **net worth**. But what if we redefined success in terms of **net joy**?

What if your budget wasn't just a plan for where your money goes, but a reflection of your values and a tool for enhancing your well-being?

This week, here's your challenge:

- Look at your past 30 days of spending.
- Categorize each transaction into three buckets: **Needs**, **Wants**, and **Joy**.
- Ask yourself: Where am I spending out of habit? Out of fear? Out of alignment?
- Where could I shift even a small percentage toward what actually makes me feel fulfilled?

Final Thought

Money is not the end goal. It's a tool. And like any tool, its value depends on how well you use it.

If you're chasing happiness through accumulation alone, you might always feel like you're coming up short. But if you focus on aligning your spending with your values, investing in experiences that matter, and giving in ways that connect you to something bigger, you might just discover you've had enough all along.

Money doesn't buy happiness—but it can fund a life that feels meaningful.

WEEK 2

Money, Identity, & Self-Worth

Let's be honest: Money is never just about math.

It's about how we feel when we walk into a room. It's the silent comparison we make to our peers. It's the reason someone might buy a luxury car they can't afford, or why another person refuses to spend on themselves even when they have more than enough.

Our relationship with money is deeply personal—and often, deeply emotional.

I grew up in a household where money was associated with security — earning it meant safety, losing it meant fear. It took me years to understand that I'd built an entire career partly to keep that fear at bay. That's not a bad thing. But knowing it changed how I worked — and how I advise.

This week is about looking in the mirror and asking a question few people take the time to explore:

How has money shaped my sense of identity and self-worth?

The Stories We Inherit

Every person carries a set of money beliefs, stories that began long before you earned your first paycheck. Maybe you grew up in a household where money was tight, and every expense came with stress. Or perhaps money was abundant, but never discussed, so you learned to associate wealth with silence or secrecy.

These early experiences lay the foundation for your "money script"—the unconscious beliefs that influence how you think, feel, and behave around money. For example:

- **"Money is security."** So you hoard it and fear spending.
- **"Money is freedom."** So you chase it endlessly.
- **"Money is a sign of success."** So you equate your worth with your net worth.

None of these beliefs are inherently wrong. But left unchecked, they can silently steer your decisions and limit your ability to feel at peace, even when your bank account says you should.

Reflection Prompt:

What were the money messages in your home growing up?

What behaviors do you repeat or resist because of those messages?

Self-Worth Vs. Net Worth

One of the most damaging ideas in modern life is the notion that our value as people is tied to our financial success. We see it everywhere—in social media, career comparisons, even casual small talk. ("What do you do?" is often just a polite way of asking, "How much status and success have you achieved?")

But equating money with self-worth creates a moving target. There's always someone who has more. A bigger house. A nicer car. A larger portfolio. And if we base our confidence on keeping up, we'll never feel "enough."

You are not your salary.

You are not your savings account.

You are not the square footage of your home or the brand of your clothes.

Real self-worth comes from something deeper—your values, your character, your contribution to the people around you. Money is a tool, not a trophy.

Unpacking Shame, Guilt, & Fear

Here's a hard truth:

For many people, money brings up **shame**.

Shame for not knowing more. For past mistakes. For credit card debt. For student loans. For not saving enough. For not earning more.

But shame thrives in secrecy. When we avoid talking about money—even with ourselves—we rob ourselves of the chance to heal and grow.

The same goes for **guilt** (spending on yourself) or **fear** (never feeling secure enough). These emotions aren't problems to be solved; they're signals. Signals that your relationship with money may be asking for some attention, honesty, and perhaps a little compassion.

Building A Healthy Financial Identity

So how do you start rewriting your money story?

Here are three practices that can help:

1. **Awareness:**
   Start noticing your emotional reactions around money. When do you feel anxiety? When do you feel confident? What situations trigger comparison or judgment?
2. **Language:**
   Change how you talk about money, even in your own head. Replace "I'm bad with money" with "I'm learning to manage money better." Language matters.
3. **Alignment:**
   The healthiest financial identity is one that reflects who you are, not who others expect you to be.

> Your spending, saving, and goals should support your values—not your insecurities.

Final Thought

Money will always be part of your story, but it doesn't have to define your worth.

You can choose to build a relationship with money that is rooted in awareness, not anxiety. In clarity, not comparison. In self-respect, not shame.

This week, your challenge is simple: write your money story. No judgment. No editing. Just honesty.

Where did your beliefs come from? What's serving you? What's holding you back? And what do you want to change moving forward?

Your relationship with money can be one of the most empowering—if you're willing to explore it honestly.

WEEK 3

Work & Purpose—Why It's Not Just About Retirement

When we talk about financial planning, especially later in life, the conversation often centers around one milestone:

Retirement.

It's painted as the finish line, the prize you get for decades of hard work. But for many people, retirement is more complicated than just stopping work. Because for many of us, **work is about more than a paycheck.**

It's about identity.

It's about purpose.

It's about routine, contribution, connection, and meaning.

This week, we're going to challenge the traditional idea of retirement—and explore what role work really plays in your life.

Work Is More Than Wages

In the financial world, we tend to reduce work to dollars and cents:

How much do you earn? How much do you need to replace?

But this view misses the emotional, psychological, and even physical benefits that work provides.

Consider what work might offer you beyond money:

- **Structure:** A reason to get up, get dressed, and engage
- **Community:** Interaction, collaboration, shared goals
- **Status:** Recognition, identity, social value
- **Purpose:** A way to contribute and create meaning

That's why many people feel **lost, bored, or even depressed** after they retire—not because they didn't plan financially, but because they didn't plan emotionally.

Retirement Isn't One-Size-Fits-All

Let's debunk a myth:

Not everyone wants (or needs) to stop working at 65.

Some people want to retire early and travel the world. Others want to keep working, but less. Some want to consult, teach, mentor, volunteer, or start something entirely new.

Retirement doesn't have to mean the absence of work. It can mean the **freedom to choose work that energizes you**, without the pressure of needing it to pay the bills.

We call this phase of life **"rewirement"**—not retiring from something, but **reconnecting to something meaningful**.

What's Your Purpose Beyond The Paycheck?

As you prepare for retirement—or even if you're decades away —now is the time to ask deeper questions:

- What do I enjoy doing, even if I'm not paid for it?
- When do I feel most energized, engaged, or useful?
- What causes or communities do I care about?
- What skills do I want to keep using—or pass on?

Money can fund your lifestyle. But purpose fuels your life. If you don't intentionally plan for both, retirement may feel empty instead of freeing.

Redefining Success In This Chapter Of Life

For much of your career, success might've been measured by

promotions, income, or achievement.

But in retirement—or pre-retirement—**the definition of success changes.**

Instead of "How much do I earn?" the more relevant questions become:

- How do I spend my time?
- Who do I spend it with?
- Am I growing, giving, and living in alignment with my values?

You may not need more money—you may need more meaning.

This isn't about abandoning ambition. It's about redirecting it.

Practical Ways To Stay Engaged After Work

If you're nearing retirement, or just want to stay mentally and emotionally active, consider:

- **Phased Retirement:** Reduce hours instead of stopping cold turkey
- **Encore Careers:** Find a second act in a new field, often values-driven
- **Advisory or Consulting Roles:** Share your wisdom without full-time commitment
- **Mentorship:** Guide younger professionals or students
- **Volunteering:** Use your skills to serve causes you care about
- **Creative Pursuits:** Writing, art, teaching, building—not for profit, but for joy

The goal is to replace what work provided: not just the income, but the **meaning.**

Final Thought

Retirement planning isn't just about money. It's about purpose.

You can have the biggest nest egg in the world and still feel adrift if you haven't thought about what comes next in terms of identity, connection, and fulfillment.

This is what I mean when I talk about rewirement. It's not the absence of work. It's the redirection of everything work gave you — structure, purpose, contribution — toward something that fits who you are now, not who you had to be.

So this week, ask yourself:

"If I didn't have to work for money, what would I want to do with my time, my talents, and my energy?"

That's the foundation of a truly fulfilling next chapter.

WEEK 4

Couples & Communication—Money Talks That Work

Money may be one of the most common reasons couples argue, but it's rarely about the numbers.

It's about communication.

Different values, spending habits, financial priorities, and emotional baggage around money can create tension, even in the healthiest relationships. One person wants to pay down the mortgage early, the other wants to travel while they're still young. One person tracks every cent, the other avoids the topic entirely.

Money fights aren't just about dollars; they're about identity, trust, control, and fear.

The good news? It doesn't have to be this way.

This week, we focus on how to have money conversations that actually bring you closer—not drive you apart.

Why Couples Struggle To Talk About Money

Here's what most people aren't taught: Money is deeply personal.

It's shaped by upbringing, life experiences, and core beliefs. When two people come together, they bring two completely different money stories into the relationship—and often assume the other person sees things the same way.

But friction is inevitable when:

- One partner is a spender, the other a saver.
- One grew up with scarcity, the other with abundance.

- One likes spreadsheets, the other likes spontaneity.

And the longer these differences go unspoken, the harder they become to navigate.

The Real Goal: Alignment, Not Agreement

You don't have to think the same way about money, but you do need to respect each other's perspectives and build a shared vision.

Financial harmony doesn't come from always agreeing. It comes from:

- Listening without judgment
- Understanding each other's "why"
- Creating a plan that reflects both partners' values

The goal isn't one person "winning" the conversation. It's working as a team.

Common Pitfalls (And How To Avoid Them)

1. Avoiding the conversation altogether
Silence creates assumptions—and assumptions erode trust. Schedule regular "money dates" to talk openly.

2. Letting one person handle all the finances
Even if one partner manages the day-to-day, both should have full visibility and a voice in decisions.

3. Getting stuck in "me vs. you" language
Shift to "we." Use phrases like "How can we align our goals?" instead of "Why did you spend that?"

4. Only talking about money when there's a problem
Don't wait until there's a crisis. Talk proactively about plans, dreams, and values.

Conversation Starters That Work

Here are a few gentle, open-ended prompts to help you get talking:

- What was money like in your family growing up?
- What financial goals matter most to you, and why?
- When do you feel most financially secure? When do you feel stressed?
- How can we support each other better with money?
- What does "financial success" look like to you?

Keep the tone curious, not critical. And remember: the point isn't to be right—it's to understand.

Building A Shared Financial Plan

Once you've opened the lines of communication, start making collaborative decisions about:

- Short- and long-term goals
- Budgeting systems
- Debt repayment
- Saving and investing
- Retirement timelines
- Big-ticket purchases

Put it in writing. Revisit it regularly. And be willing to adjust as life changes.

Final Thought

Money is not a math problem for couples to solve. It's a relationship skill to be practiced.

If money has been a source of friction, you're not alone. But with honesty, empathy, and teamwork, it can become a source of connection.

Money talks don't have to be hard. They just have to happen.

And the more you talk, the easier they become.

Action Step:

Plan a 30-minute "money date" with your partner this week. Use one of the conversation starters above. Set the intention to listen, not fix. End by celebrating one thing you're doing well together.

◆◆◆

Wrapping Up September

Numbers are only part of the story. By exploring where your money beliefs came from, how they shape your decisions, and how to align your spending with what you actually value, you've done work most people never do. That's worth something.

Next month, we move from the inner work to the legal framework — making sure the life you've built, and the people you love, are protected when it matters most.

Client Convos: Relationships With Money

I had a client — first-generation, second-generation family — whose parents had kept all their money in cash. Literally. Shoeboxes, cupboards, hidden in corners of the house. No bank accounts. No investments. All cash, all the time.

He had inherited that relationship with money. No debt, no investments, no financial system — everything in cash. It felt safe to him. It was all he'd ever known.
When I showed him the opportunity cost — what that money could have been doing for him, how many additional years he'd have to work because his money simply wasn't working at all — it landed hard. It took time.

You don't undo a lifetime of learned behavior in a single meeting. But he trusted the process. He made the shift. And today he's one of our great success stories — he was able to retire half a dozen years earlier than he would have otherwise. Not because anything dramatic changed in his income or his expenses. Because his money finally started working.

OCTOBER - MONTH 10

If You Don't Plan, Someone Else Will—For Better or Worse

Estate planning is one of those topics that's easy to put off. It feels distant, maybe even morbid. You tell yourself you'll get to it after the next big life event—after the kids graduate, after retirement, after things calm down. But here's the truth: If you don't plan for what happens to your assets, your family, and your wishes, someone else will do it for you. And it might not turn out the way you'd want.

Without a clear estate plan, your financial legacy gets handed over to courts, state laws, and a legal system that doesn't know you or what matters most to you. Decisions that should reflect your values, your relationships, and your intentions become dictated by default rules. That can lead to delays, confusion, and unnecessary costs—but more importantly, it can lead to real emotional and financial stress for your loved ones.

This month is about reclaiming control. Estate planning isn't just for the ultra-wealthy. It's for anyone who cares about what happens to their family, their finances, and their future. Whether you're a single parent with young kids, an empty nester downsizing for retirement, or somewhere in between, this is your opportunity to make your wishes clear and legally enforceable.

But estate planning is about more than wills and trusts. It's also about making sure someone you trust can make healthcare or financial decisions if you're unable to. It's about protecting your family from elder scams, preventing unnecessary legal battles, and leaving behind clarity instead of chaos.

In April, we introduced the essential documents every adult needs. This month, we go further — exploring how to protect those decisions, communicate them to your family, and use advanced tools like trusts to preserve what you've built.

You've worked hard to build a life and a legacy. This is the part of your financial plan that ensures what you've built is protected, and that your values carry on, even if you're no longer here to speak for yourself.

Let's walk through what it means to build a thoughtful, effective estate plan—one that reflects not just what you have, but who you are, and what matters most to you.

WEEK 1

Why Estate Planning Isn't Just For The Wealthy

You might already have a will. Maybe you've named your beneficiaries and assigned a Power of Attorney. That's a solid start — and if April motivated you to get those basics in place, that's exactly what it was designed to do.

But having documents isn't the same as having a plan.

A plan means those documents are current, accessible, and understood by the people who need to act on them. It means someone you trust can step in — financially and medically — if you're unable to speak for yourself. It means your family won't be left guessing, grieving, and navigating a legal system that doesn't know you, all at the same time.

That's what this month is about.

Why "No Plan" Is Still A Plan (It's Actually Someone Else's Problem)

If you die without a will, the state doesn't leave your estate in limbo — it distributes it for you. That process is called intestate succession, and it follows a fixed legal pecking order that has no way of accounting for blended families, estranged relatives, long-term partners who never married, or close friends who feel like family. It doesn't reflect your values. It doesn't know your story.

The same gap exists if you become incapacitated. Without the right documents in place, even a spouse can face legal hurdles accessing accounts, authorizing medical care, or managing day-to-day finances during a crisis. Courts may need to appoint a guardian — a process that is slow, public, and expensive — when you could have simply named someone you trust.

Estate Planning Is For Everyone

You don't need a large estate to need a plan. If you have a bank account, a retirement fund, a car, children, or preferences about your own medical care — you have an estate. And the people you love deserve clarity, not confusion, when the time comes.

This month, we'll go beyond the basics — exploring how to protect your decisions, communicate them to your family, and use the right tools to make sure what you've built transfers the way you intend.

Action Step:

Pull out whatever estate documents you currently have.

Ask yourself three questions:
Are they current?
Do the right people know where to find them?
And does anyone in your life know what role they've been asked to play?

If the answer to any of those is no — that's where we start.

WEEK 2

Planning For The Unexpected

If the past few years have taught us anything, it's this: Life is unpredictable. One day everything is normal, the next it's anything but. And while we can't control the future, we can prepare for it, especially when it comes to our health, our voice, and the people we trust.

Estate planning isn't just about what happens after you die. Some of the most important documents you'll ever create are those that protect you *while* you're still alive.

This week, we're talking about planning for incapacity—that uncomfortable, often-overlooked area of estate planning that can have huge consequences. Because if you can't speak for yourself, who will?

The Power Of A Plan

Imagine being in a car accident or having a medical emergency that leaves you unconscious or unable to communicate. Or maybe you're in surgery and a decision needs to be made—fast. In moments like these, your family might be forced to guess what you would've wanted. Worse, they could disagree, leading to conflict at the worst possible time.

This is where advance directives come in.

These documents ensure your wishes are known and respected. They empower someone you trust to step in and help when you can't help yourself.

Let's break down the three most essential tools:

1. Healthcare Power Of Attorney

This document designates someone—your agent—to make medical decisions on your behalf if you're unable to do so. They don't have power over your finances or property, just your healthcare. You choose who this is. You can change it at any time. And they can speak on your behalf if you're incapacitated.

Why it matters: Without a healthcare POA, the default decision-maker might be a next-of-kin who doesn't know your wishes, or worse, who disagrees with them.

2. Living Will (Advance Directive)

A living will is a legal document that outlines your preferences for end-of-life care. This can include decisions around life-sustaining treatment, resuscitation (DNR orders), ventilators, feeding tubes, and organ donation.

Why it matters: A living will takes the pressure off your loved ones during an emotional time. They don't have to guess or carry the weight of these decisions—they just follow your guidance.

3. Health Insurance Portability And Accountability Act Authorization

This allows medical professionals to share your health information with the people you designate. Without it, even your spouse or children may be denied access to updates about your condition or treatment.

Why it matters: Without a signed HIPAA release, your loved ones may be shut out of crucial conversations during a medical crisis.

Who Should Have These Documents?

Short answer: Everyone over the age of 18.

That's right. As soon as a child becomes a legal adult, parents no longer have automatic access to their medical records or decision-making authority. College students. Single adults. Married couples. Retirees. Business owners. Everyone needs a plan.

These documents are especially critical for:

- **Single adults** without a default spouse or partner to make decisions
- **Blended families** where family dynamics may be complex
- **People with chronic illnesses** or those who want to avoid aggressive treatment
- **Same-sex couples** or long-term partners who may not have legal recognition in every state

When Life Changes, Update Your Plan

Life evolves—and so should your documents. Review and update your healthcare directives and powers of attorney after major milestones like:

- Marriage or divorce
- Birth of a child or grandchild
- Diagnosis of a serious illness
- Death of a previously named agent
- Relocation to a different state

Start The Conversation Now

Talking about these things may feel awkward or overwhelming, but it's one of the most loving and responsible conversations you can have. It gives clarity, control, and peace of mind—for you and the people who care about you.

Consider this your permission to plan. Remember that control isn't about obsessing over every possibility. It's about having a plan in place that reflects your voice, even when you can't speak.

Next week, we'll explore how to keep what you've built out of the probate process and protected from unnecessary complications.

WEEK 3

Avoiding Probate & Protecting What You've Built

You've worked hard to build a life, a family, and a future. You've saved, invested, and planned. But without proper legal documents in place, everything you've built could get tied up in one of the slowest, costliest, and most public legal processes out there: probate.

This week is about protecting what you've worked so hard for—not just from taxes or lawsuits, but from delays, disputes, and red tape. Because estate planning isn't only about *what* you leave behind; it's about *how* it gets passed on.

Let's start by understanding what probate is—and why you might want to avoid it.

What Is Probate?

Probate is the legal process through which a deceased person's assets are inventoried, debts are settled, and remaining property is distributed to heirs.

That might sound simple, but probate can be:

- **Time-consuming:** It often lasts 9–18 months or longer.
- **Expensive:** Attorney fees, court costs, and administrative expenses can eat up a significant portion of your estate.
- **Public:** Probate is a matter of public record, which means anyone can access information about your assets, debts, and beneficiaries.
- **Stressful:** Heirs often face delays, confusion, and sometimes even conflict.

Common Probate Triggers

You might assume that having a will means you'll avoid probate. Unfortunately, that's a common misconception. A will *still goes through probate*—it just gives the court instructions to follow.

The real key to avoiding probate is *how* your assets are titled and whether they automatically transfer to your heirs.

Assets that typically go through probate include:

- Individually owned real estate
- Bank and brokerage accounts with no beneficiary listed
- Personal property like jewelry, vehicles, and collectibles
- Business interests without succession plans

Ways To Avoid Probate

The good news is, you can take proactive steps now to simplify—or avoid—probate for your heirs.

Here's how:

1. Use Beneficiary Designations

Accounts like IRAs, 401(k)s, life insurance, and even some bank accounts allow you to name a beneficiary or transfer-on-death (TOD) designation. This allows the asset to pass *directly* to your chosen person, bypassing probate.

Bonus tip: Review your beneficiaries regularly. Life changes, such as divorces, marriages, or deaths, can make outdated designations a problem.

2. Create A Revocable Living Trust

A trust allows you to move your assets out of your name and into the name of the trust, while still permitting you to maintain control during your lifetime. When you pass away, the trust distributes your assets according to your instructions *without going through probate.*

Trusts are especially helpful if you:

- Own property in multiple states
- Have minor children or dependents with special needs
- Want to protect your heirs from creditors, lawsuits, or divorce
- Prefer to keep your affairs private

3. Consider Joint Ownership With Rights Of Survivorship

For some assets, jointly owning property (with a spouse, for example) allows it to pass directly to the surviving owner.

4. Explore Small Estate Affidavits

If the value of your estate is under a certain threshold (which varies by state), your heirs may be able to use a simplified process to access your assets—but this is only an option in limited cases.

Trusts: More Than Just A Tool For The Wealthy

Many people assume that trusts are only for the ultra-wealthy. Not true.

Trusts are useful for anyone who wants to:

- Maintain control over how and when their assets are used
- Provide for heirs with special needs or spending issues
- Protect heirs from future lawsuits, creditors, or bad marriages
- Reduce the risk of family conflict or court intervention

One powerful benefit? **Asset protection.** When set up correctly, certain types of trusts can shield assets from being accessed in divorce settlements or lawsuits against your beneficiaries.

Take Action: Protect What You've Built

You've spent your life building a financial foundation. Now it's time to put up guardrails to ensure it transfers efficiently, privately, and in line with your values.

- Review your assets and how they're titled.
- Name beneficiaries where appropriate.
- Talk to an estate planning attorney about whether a trust makes sense for you.

Next week, we'll talk about how to protect the people *inside* your plan—not just the assets—by creating safety nets for your family in times of vulnerability or crisis.

WEEK 4

The Most Important Conversation You'll Ever Have

By this point, you've taken critical steps: created a will, assigned powers of attorney, reviewed beneficiaries, and considered trusts. But there's one piece of estate planning that many people still overlook—**communicating your plan**.

And in many cases, this single omission does the most damage.

Estate documents are legal tools. But legacy is emotional. If your loved ones are left guessing—or worse, shocked—by your choices after you're gone, no set of perfectly worded legal forms will fix that. That's why this week is about opening the lines of communication *while you still can.*

Let's call it what it is: a difficult conversation. You're talking about your death, about money, about decisions your family might not agree with. But it's also one of the most caring, responsible, and loving things you can do.

Why Transparency Matters More Than You Think

Estate plans often follow a typical structure: Everything goes to the spouse, and then to children in equal shares. But what if your situation is more nuanced? What if:

- One child is more financially secure than another
- You've remarried and have a blended family
- You want to leave a portion to charity
- You've included—or excluded—certain people for personal reasons

These are valid and common situations. But they can lead to

confusion, resentment, or even legal disputes if your loved ones don't understand your intentions.

Clarity now prevents conflict later.

In fact, one of the biggest regrets we hear from heirs is: *"I wish I knew why they made that decision."* Unanswered questions don't disappear. They linger.

What To Share (And With Whom)

You don't need to provide exact dollar amounts or copies of every document, but you should give your loved ones a clear sense of:

- The structure of your estate plan
- Who is receiving what, and why
- Who you've appointed for key roles (executor, Power of Attorney, trustee)
- How to access important information if something happens to you

Even a basic conversation can dramatically reduce future stress. But the more detail you can offer, the better.

This isn't about justification—it's about context.

If you've made a nontraditional decision (e.g., leaving more to one child, giving to a cause, excluding someone), explain it directly or in writing. As I've shared in my blog, this small act of communication can prevent lifelong rifts between siblings, children, or spouses.

If You Can't Say It In Person, Leave A Letter Or Video

Not everyone feels comfortable having this conversation face-to-face, and that's okay. You can still preserve your intent and protect your relationships by writing a **"letter of intent"** or recording a short video to accompany your will.

This isn't a legal document. It's a personal one.

Your letter can explain:

- The reasoning behind your estate plan
- Your values and hopes for your heirs
- Any personal messages or wisdom you want to pass on

A video adds even more emotional clarity—your tone, voice, and expression can all convey what words on a page might miss.

Think of this as your opportunity to leave not just assets, but understanding.

How To Start The Conversation

Talking about death is hard. Talking about money can be even harder. But you don't have to launch into a PowerPoint presentation at Thanksgiving.

Here are some simple ways to begin:

- "I recently updated my will, and I want you to understand what's in it."
- "If something were to happen to me, I don't want you to be caught off guard."
- "This plan reflects what I value—and I want you to hear it from me, not from a document."

You can also involve your advisor or estate attorney if you'd like a neutral third party to facilitate the discussion.

Final Thought: The Legacy Of Communication

In the end, your estate plan is more than a set of instructions. It's a reflection of your life, your love, and your values.

By having this conversation, you're giving your family more

than clarity. You're giving them peace. You're showing them that this plan was made with intention and care, not secrecy or surprise.

Your voice matters. Make sure it's heard—now, not later.

Action Step:

Write a short letter—or record a two-minute video—explaining your estate plan and your intentions. If you've made any decisions that might raise questions, address them directly. Then, schedule a conversation with your family. It doesn't need to be formal. It just needs to happen.

◆ ◆ ◆

Wrapping Up October

An estate plan isn't a morbid task — it's an act of love. By putting the right documents in place and starting the right conversations, you've taken care of the people who matter most, even for the moments you won't be there for.

Next month, we go beyond the documents. November is about legacy — not just what you leave behind, but what it means, and how to make sure it carries your values forward.

Client Convos: Estate Planning and Special Needs

I received a referral for a husband and wife in a particularly difficult situation. The husband had already passed. The wife was alive, but terminally ill. They had an adult child with special needs — and when they brought me their estate planning documents, I immediately saw the problem.

There was no special needs trust. The way the estate was structured, their child — who qualified for critical government subsidies and support programs — would have received an inheritance that would have disqualified her from all of it. The very money meant to protect her would have stripped away the safety net she depended on.

We moved fast. New documents were drafted and executed. About a month later, the wife passed. Because of the planning we'd rushed into place, their daughter's future was protected exactly the way her parents had always intended. One month. That's all the time there was. And it was enough — because someone caught it in time.

NOVEMBER - MONTH 11

Legacy & Impact

What Do You Want To Leave Behind—And How Should It Be Received?

My father, 'Pop-E' as we called him, didn't leave behind a large estate. What he left behind was something harder to put a number on — a sense of how to show up for the people you love. When I think about legacy now, I think about him. Not the money. The presence.

When we hear the word legacy, our minds jump to estates, wills, and inheritances. But legacy is far bigger—and far richer—than money. It's the values you taught. The memories you created. The impact you made on lives you touched.

Legacy isn't just a transfer at the end of life; it's the story you're writing now.

Reframing Legacy

Your legacy is not simply what you leave behind—it's **how** it's received. Are your heirs confused? Entitled? Grateful and aligned with your values?

Intentional legacy planning shifts the narrative from "what gets left" to "what gets understood, honored, and carried forward."

Why Legacy Planning Gets Avoided

Talking about what happens *after* you're gone can feel uncomfortable.

- You might think, **"I'm not rich enough"** and wrongly postpone planning.
- You might fear creating conflict or sacrificing privacy.
- Or you might simply assume **"my loved ones will know what to do."**

Yet avoidance leaves your family with ambiguity, delays, and stress. Without your input, your legacy lands in the probate system, unclear about what you hoped for.

The Value Of Intentional Planning

When you plan intentionally, you give your family clarity, your values a voice, and your financial life a purpose beyond accumulation.

You:

- Reduce the potential for misunderstandings or conflict.
- Make your wishes clear, not just in documents but in stories.
- Connect the assets you've built with the values you've lived.
- Create peace of mind—not just for you, but for those

you leave behind.

Reflection Prompt:

I ask this question in client meetings all the time. My own answer has shifted over the years. For a long time it was about the firm — what we built, how many families we served. Now it's simpler. I want my kids to remember that I was present. That's the whole thing.

Here's your starting question:

"What do I want to be remembered for?"

Pause. Consider the answer.

- Is it about the careers you pursued?
- The way you treated others?
- The causes you supported?
- The freedom and values you passed to your children or grandchildren?

Write it down. This is not a checklist—it's a foundation.

Your legacy isn't just what happens one day. It's how you live, give, and lead every year.

WEEK 1

Leaving Money To Family & Charities

When it comes to legacy, money is often the first thing people think of, but it's rarely the most important. What matters isn't just **what** you leave behind, but **how** it's received. A thoughtful financial legacy can be a gift of clarity, confidence, and continuity. A disorganized one? It can leave confusion, resentment, and missed opportunities.

This week is about how to be deliberate in the financial gifts you leave—both to family and to causes you care about—so they reflect your values and avoid unintended consequences.

Structuring Financial Gifts Thoughtfully

Whether you're leaving money to children, grandchildren, or other loved ones, one of the most important decisions you'll make is **how** they receive it.

1. Lump-Sum Inheritance

It's the simplest method: A beneficiary receives the entire amount all at once. This approach works best when:

- The recipient is financially responsible
- The gift is relatively modest
- You want to minimize administrative complexity

But lump sums can backfire. Sudden wealth—especially when unexpected—can be overwhelming. Many people spend windfalls quickly without lasting benefit.

2. Staggered Distributions

Also known as **structured inheritance**, this strategy allows you to distribute funds in phases:

- A portion at age 25
- Another at 30
- The rest at 35, for example

This gives heirs time to grow into their financial responsibility and can prevent major missteps in early adulthood.

3. Incentive-Based Trusts

Want to encourage certain values or behaviors? You can structure trusts that release funds based on:

- Graduating from college
- Maintaining employment
- Avoiding criminal activity
- Completing drug or alcohol rehab

Incentive trusts are powerful, but they must be designed carefully to avoid being punitive or overly controlling.

Strategic Giving To Charities

Leaving money to charity doesn't just support causes you care about—it can also be a strategic move for reducing taxes and building a purpose-driven legacy.

Donor-Advised Funds

Think of a DAF as a charitable investment account. You contribute money, receive an immediate tax deduction, and then recommend grants to your favorite nonprofits over time.

DAFs are:

- Easy to set up
- Flexible in timing
- Great for involving family in giving decisions

Charitable Trusts

Charitable trusts can be powerful tools for giving strategically while also supporting income or legacy goals. Two common structures—the Charitable Remainder Trust (CRT) and the Charitable Lead Trust (CLT)—work in opposite ways but are equally useful depending on your objectives.

Charitable Remainder Trust

A CRT provides income to you (or another beneficiary) for a set number of years or for life. When the trust ends, the remaining assets go to charity.

Income to you now → charity later.

Benefits Include:

- Creating a lifetime or term income stream
- Diversifying appreciated assets tax-efficiently
- Supporting charities you care about
- Providing potential tax deductions and planning opportunities

Charitable Lead Trust

A CLT works in the reverse. The charity receives income from the trust first, for a defined term. When the trust ends, the remaining assets go to your heirs.

Income to charity now → heirs later.

Benefits Include:

- Reducing the taxable value of your estate
- Supporting charitable causes during your lifetime
- Passing assets to heirs at a potentially lower transfer-tax cost

In short:
CRT = *you now, charity later*
CLT = *charity now, heirs later*

Used intentionally, these trusts allow you to align giving, income, and legacy in a way that reflects your values.

Talking About The "Why" Behind Your Giving

One of the most overlooked parts of legacy planning is **explaining your intent**.

Why this cause?

Why this amount?

Why now?

When family members understand the values behind your decisions, they're less likely to second-guess them—and more likely to carry them forward.

Some families or individuals choose to write a **Legacy Letter** or record a video sharing:

- What causes mattered most to them and why
- Hopes for how future generations will continue their impact
- The reasoning behind giving decisions (charitable or otherwise)

These messages can be more powerful than any dollar

amount.

Aligning Your Bequests With Your Purpose

The goal isn't to simply "give money away." It's to leave a legacy that reflects **who you are and what you believe in**. That might mean:

- Creating a scholarship fund in your hometown
- Supporting an organization that helped you or your family
- Funding a family foundation that gives your descendants a shared mission

Legacy is about intention. The more clearly your financial gifts align with your purpose, the more powerful they become.

Action Step:

Write down one charitable cause and one family member you'd want to include in your legacy. Then, jot down how you'd want each to be supported—and why. This is the beginning of a legacy plan that's not just generous, but meaningful.

WEEK 2

Should You Talk To Your Heirs? (Yes.)

It's one of the most common mistakes in estate and legacy planning: doing the paperwork, but skipping the conversation.

Too often, people assume that avoiding the topic will prevent family tension. They think, "My wishes are in writing. That's enough." But the truth is, secrecy creates more confusion, not less. And silence leaves room for assumptions, disappointment, and even resentment.

Talking to your heirs while you're alive doesn't weaken your legacy. It strengthens it.

Why Secrecy Backfires

When families don't talk about inheritance plans ahead of time, here's what tends to happen:

- Adult children are blindsided by what they receive—or don't.
- Loved ones misunderstand your intentions and assume favoritism.
- Siblings squabble over assets or sentimental items.
- Your values and reasoning are lost in translation.

What could have been a final act of love and clarity becomes a source of confusion and hurt.

Only **24% of Americans have a will**, and even fewer have discussed their wishes with their family. This gap leaves a vacuum that emotions, rumors, and disagreements quickly fill.

What The Conversation Can Achieve

Done well, talking to your heirs about your legacy plan can:

- **Reduce surprises** and manage expectations
- **Explain the "why"** behind your choices—financial and personal
- **Clarify logistics** around key roles (executor, POA, trustee)
- **Empower your heirs** to make informed decisions about their own planning
- **Demonstrate care** by making things easier, not harder, in your absence

How To Start The Conversation

Bringing up your estate plan doesn't have to be a dramatic or formal event. In fact, it's often better when it's casual, open, and framed as a gift, not a burden.

Here are a few ways to begin:

If You're Nervous:

"I've been working on some planning lately and realized I haven't shared much about it with you. Can we talk about what I've put in place and why?"

If You Want To Frame It As Preparation:

"I hope none of this will matter for a long time, but I want to make sure there's no confusion down the road. I've made some decisions and just want you to be in the loop."

If You've Named Them In Your Plan:

"I've asked you to take on a role—executor, healthcare proxy, etc.—and I want to make sure you're comfortable and clear on what it means."

This isn't about defending your choices. It's about giving context, easing future stress, and offering peace of mind.

Navigating Difficult Family Dynamics

Every family is different. Maybe there's tension, estrangement, or financial inequality between siblings. Maybe you're worried that your decisions will disappoint someone. That's exactly why these conversations matter.

Here are a few principles to guide you:

- **Be honest but kind.** You don't need to share every number, but transparency builds trust.
- **Stick to your values.** Explain the *why*, even if it's uncomfortable.
- **Avoid comparing.** Frame your decisions individually, not in relation to others.
- **Consider a facilitator.** If your family dynamics are complex, involving a financial advisor, estate attorney, or even a counselor can help.

Setting Expectations, Not Entitlements

Talking about your legacy is not the same as promising an inheritance. It's about aligning your values, clarifying intentions, and removing guesswork. You might say:

"We've tried to create a plan that reflects what's most important to us—caring for each other, giving back, and minimizing conflict. I want you to understand how we got here, even if every decision isn't perfect."

A Final Thought

The greatest legacy isn't just what you leave behind; it's how you leave it.

Don't let your silence become someone else's burden. Don't assume your paperwork can speak for you. Take the time to have the conversation. It may be uncomfortable in the moment, but it's a lasting gift of clarity, connection, and care.

Action Step:

Schedule a conversation with your loved ones about your legacy plan. Choose a setting that feels natural: around the dinner table, on a walk, or during a family gathering. You don't need to disclose every detail, just open the door.

You've worked hard to build a meaningful life. Make sure your legacy carries that meaning forward, with your voice, your presence, and your intention.

WEEK 3

Caring For Aging Parents—Planning With Empathy And Clarity

At some point in your life, the roles begin to reverse. The people who raised you, cared for you, and made countless sacrifices for your future now need your help navigating their own. This stage can arrive gradually, or all at once—with a fall, a diagnosis, or a phone call that changes everything.

And when it does, many people find themselves in the middle of the so-called "sandwich generation": raising children while also supporting aging parents. It's a season of financial strain, emotional complexity, and often logistical overwhelm.

But it can also be a time of deep connection, clarity, and compassion—if you're prepared.

This week is about planning for your parents' aging years with the same intentionality you bring to your own financial future. It's not just about money. It's about dignity, autonomy, and making sure your family has the support it needs when it matters most.

The Emotional Landscape: Stress, Guilt, And Gratitude

Caring for parents while managing your own household is no small feat. It can surface a complex mix of emotions:

- **Guilt** about not doing enough, or needing to set boundaries
- **Resentment** over uneven responsibility among siblings

- **Gratitude** for the opportunity to give back
- **Grief** as you begin to lose aspects of the person they used to be

These emotions are normal. But without a plan, they can spiral into tension and burnout.

Planning isn't just about logistics. It's about protecting your family's emotional well-being by reducing confusion, sharing responsibility, and ensuring your parents' wishes are honored.

The Financial Realities: What You Need To Know

Caring for aging parents often comes with unexpected costs. According to AARP, 78% of family caregivers incur out-of-pocket expenses, averaging over $7,000 per year.

Start by understanding their full financial picture:

- **What are their income sources?** Social Security, pensions, investment income?
- **Do they have long-term care insurance or health coverage beyond Medicare?**
- **What are their ongoing monthly expenses, and do they have any debts?**
- **Do they have a financial advisor, CPA, or attorney you can connect with?**

Then, consider how their needs might evolve:

- Home modifications?
- In-home care?
- Assisted living or skilled nursing?

The earlier you assess these realities, the better prepared you'll be to help them transition with stability and dignity.

Legal Tools That Make Life Easier Later

One of the most painful experiences families face is being unprepared when a parent loses capacity.

Avoid that heartache by making sure the following documents are in place—and current:

1. **Financial Power of Attorney (POA)**

o This allows someone (ideally a trusted child or advisor) to manage financial affairs if your parent becomes incapacitated.

o Without it, you may need court approval to access accounts or make basic decisions.

2. **Healthcare Proxy/Medical POA**

o This designates someone to make medical decisions if your parent can't.

o It should align with your parent's stated wishes about treatment preferences.

3. **Living Will/Advance Directive**

o This documents preferences for life-sustaining measures.

o It relieves loved ones from having to guess or make emotionally fraught decisions in moments of crisis.

4. **HIPAA Authorization**

o This grants you access to medical records, which is essential for navigating care.

5. **Will and/or Trust**

o These establish how assets should be distributed.

o Trusts can also help manage finances during a parent's lifetime, especially if cognitive decline is an issue.

Sharing The Load: Family Dynamics And Communication

In many families, one sibling becomes the default caregiver

due to geography, availability, or relationship dynamics. This often creates friction, especially if others aren't contributing equally or are unaware of the daily burden.

Here are some ways to address it:

- **Hold a family meeting** (virtual or in person) to discuss roles, resources, and expectations.
- **Assign responsibilities** based on strengths. One sibling may handle finances, another logistics, another emotional support.
- **Be transparent** about costs, time commitments, and emotional impact.
- **Use shared tools** like a Google Doc or care coordination app to keep everyone informed.

You don't need perfect alignment—but you do need communication.

Start The Conversation Now

It may feel awkward to bring this up with your parents. But waiting until there's a crisis only makes it harder.

Try gentle prompts like:

- "Have you ever thought about how you'd want to be cared for if something happened?"
- "Do you have anyone you've designated to help with medical or financial decisions if you couldn't?"
- "Would it be helpful for us to look over things together so we're not scrambling later on?"

Frame it as an act of love, not control. Most parents don't want to burden their kids—but without a plan, the burden is inevitable.

Action Step:

Schedule time this week to talk with your parents about their current situation and future wishes. Start with one topic—like healthcare preferences or financial accounts—and build from there. If you have siblings, loop them in. And if your parents are resistant, remind them that planning ahead protects, rather than threatens, their independence.

WEEK 4

Trust Planning, Gifting, And Avoiding Surprises

If estate planning is about protecting the people you love, then trust planning and gifting are the tools that help you do it on your terms. This week, we'll explore how to use trusts to shape your legacy, how to give strategically during your lifetime, and why transparency now can save your family heartache later.

Why Trusts Matter—And When To Use Them

Many people think of trusts as something only the ultra-wealthy need. But in reality, a well-structured trust can be a powerful planning tool for families at a wide range of asset levels. A trust gives you control over how, when, and to whom your assets are distributed.

Here's a quick overview of the main types:

- **Revocable Living Trust:** You retain control of the assets during your lifetime and can make changes or dissolve the trust. It helps your estate avoid probate and keeps your affairs private.
- **Irrevocable Trust:** Once established, you generally can't change or dissolve it. But it offers benefits like asset protection, estate tax reduction, and shielded gifting.
- **Testamentary Trust:** This trust is created through your will and only goes into effect after your death. It can provide structure for minor children, loved ones with special needs, or beneficiaries who aren't ready for a lump sum inheritance.

Trusts allow you to stagger distributions (e.g., one-third at age 30, another at 40), provide incentives (e.g., graduate college or stay sober to access funds), or protect assets from divorce, lawsuits, or poor financial habits.

Think of it as giving with guardrails.

Smart Gifting Strategies

Giving while you're alive can be one of the most rewarding parts of your legacy plan. But doing it thoughtfully can also reduce your taxable estate and provide help when it's most needed.

Here are key strategies:

•**Annual Exclusion Gifts:** These numbers change each year. Visit irs.gov for the current year limits.

•**Lifetime Gift Tax Exemption:** The lifetime gift tax exemption has been historically high in recent years — consult your advisor or IRS.gov for the current figure, as this number changes annually and is subject to legislative adjustments. For married couples, the exemption is generally double the individual amount. Large gifts made during high-exemption years may reduce your taxable estate and lock in today's limits.

•**Education and Medical Gifts:** You can pay tuition or medical expenses directly to an institution without using your annual exclusion. It's a great way to help grandchildren or other loved ones.

•**Five-Year 529 Superfunding:** Some families choose to "superfund" a 529 plan by contributing up to five years' worth of the annual gift exclusion all at once. This strategy can help front-load education savings and maximize potential market growth. Because the annual gift exclusion amount changes over time, the exact superfunding limit also changes. Before making a large contribution, check the current IRS guidelines or talk with your advisor to ensure you're within the allowable limits.

•**Special Needs Trusts:** If you're supporting a loved one with a disability, a special needs trust helps protect their benefits while ensuring they have access to additional support.

A well-designed gifting plan reflects both your capacity to give and your intention behind it. Don't just think in dollars—think in impact.

Pitfalls To Avoid

Even the best intentions can backfire if not planned with care. Some of the most common estate planning landmines include:

- **Unequal Treatment Without Explanation:** If one child receives more than another—or gets different types of assets—be clear about why. Silence invites resentment.
- **Secret Accounts or Surprise Gifts:** These often create confusion and hurt feelings, especially when discovered after your passing. Transparency beats secrecy every time.
- **Last-Minute Decisions:** Updating your estate plan too close to death can trigger legal challenges or raise questions about your intentions. Aim for proactivity, not panic.

Your plan doesn't need to be perfect. But it does need to be clear, fair, and consistent with your values.

Why Surprises Usually Backfire

Many people avoid discussing their estate plans because they fear conflict or awkwardness. But in most cases, not talking about it creates more confusion, not less.

When your heirs know your intentions—and the reasons behind them—they're less likely to feel blindsided or hurt. They're more likely to respect your decisions, even if they don't fully agree.

Sharing your plan isn't about seeking approval. It's about preserving family harmony.

Final Thought

Trusts and gifting aren't just financial tools. They're relationship tools. They allow you to care for your loved ones in thoughtful, intentional ways, now and in the future.

A strong estate plan is a reflection of your values, not just your valuables. And the more intentional you are about how you give, the more meaningful your legacy becomes.

Action Step:

Meet with your estate attorney or advisor to review your current trust and gifting strategies. Are your documents aligned with your wishes? Are your beneficiaries aware of what to expect? Write a one-page "legacy letter" explaining the why behind your plan. It could be the most important document you leave behind.

Wrapping Up November

Legacy isn't built in a single document — it's built in decades of decisions, conversations, and the values you live every day. This month, you've started thinking about what you want to leave behind, and more importantly, how you want it to be received.

Next month, we close the year with intention — exploring how giving, in all its forms, can be one of the most meaningful financial decisions you make.

Client Convos: Legacy Beyond Wealth

I had a client who wanted to set up a charitable foundation. What made it remarkable was that he wasn't wealthy by the standards you'd typically associate with that kind of move. A decent estate, nothing extraordinary on paper.

But he had identified a local school district and a cause he believed in. His plan was to fund a scholarship — not with a large lump sum, but with a permanent endowment that would generate interest every year, around ten thousand dollars annually, disbursed as scholarship money. In perpetuity.

It will outlast him. It will outlast anyone who knew him. Students who were born decades after he's gone will receive that scholarship and never know his name — but they'll be changed by it. That's a legacy. Not a tax strategy. Not an estate plan. A legacy. And it came from someone most people would have looked at and said: they probably don't need this kind of planning.

DECEMBER - MONTH 12

Charitable Giving & Year-End Planning

As the year draws to a close, many of us feel a mix of reflection, relief, and responsibility. We look at the calendar and realize that time is slipping away—along with opportunities to make meaningful financial decisions. At that moment, the notion of giving often surfaces. But most of the time, it's reactive: We hear the year-end donation deadline ticking, we get a holiday charity appeal, we think about taxes at the last minute.

What if instead, your giving was purposeful: planned with intention, aligned with your values, and integrated into your broader financial life? What if generosity wasn't just a holiday tradition, but a strategic move that amplifies both impact and meaning?

I've watched giving change people. Not just the organizations they give to — the givers themselves. There's something that happens when generosity becomes a habit rather than an annual tax decision. People who give consistently carry themselves differently. I've seen it too many times to think it's a coincidence.

Reframe Giving As A Strategy, Not Just An Emotional Act

Generosity has always come from the heart, and it should. The true beauty of giving lies in the feeling of connection, compassion, and contribution. But when we pair that feeling with thoughtful planning, we unlock something far greater: generosity that works for you, your loved ones, and the causes you believe in.

For example:

- A contribution to a cause you care about becomes more than a gift; it becomes a statement of your values.
- A donation timed at year-end becomes not just a tax deduction, but part of your legacy strategy.
- Involving your children in family giving decisions becomes a way to transfer not just wealth, but ethos.

Giving isn't just a financial act — it's an identity-building one. When generosity becomes habitual, it shifts from something you *do* to part of who you *are*. Meaningful giving reinforces your values, strengthens your sense of purpose, and deepens your connection to something larger than yourself.

The Dual Benefits: Emotional And Financial

Let's talk about both sides of the equation:

Emotional Benefits

- Giving feels good—it creates joy, connection, and purpose. Research shows that people who give generously also report higher levels of well-being.
- Giving creates stories. Imagine telling your grandchild

about the scholarship fund you started, or how you contributed to a community project because you believed in it.

- Giving builds identity. When you make giving a habit, it becomes part of who you are, not just what you do.

Financial Benefits

- Donations reduce your taxable income (when structured properly).
- Certain vehicles allow you to give and retain flexibility (donor-advised funds, charitable trusts).
- Giving strategically at year-end means you can take advantage of deadlines, maximize deductions, and plan for the upcoming year.

Aligning Giving With Purpose And Tax Strategy

To give effectively—meaningfully and wisely—you must answer two questions: *What matters to me?* and *How can I make it work within my financial plan?*

1. **What matters to me?**
    - Which causes or communities have touched your life?
    - What values do you want to express with your giving—justice, education, environment, health, family?
    - What kind of impact do you want your philanthropy to have?
2. **How can I make it work?**
    - What are the most tax-efficient ways to donate? (An example is donating appreciated stock—leveraging QCDs if you're 70½+

—using donor-advised funds. The maximum QCD amount is indexed for inflation each year, so check the IRS for the current limit.)

  - How does this gift affect your year-end financial plan (taxes, cash flow, charitable dreams)?
  - How can your giving plan connect with your family—inviting participation, sharing stories, creating a legacy?

Reflection Prompt:

"What kind of impact do I want my giving to have?"

Take a moment. Sit quietly. Think about giving you've done in the past and how it made you feel. Then ask:

- If I could choose one cause to support this year, right now, which one would it be?
- If I could involve one family member in that decision, who would it be—and why?
- What story might my grandchildren tell about the generosity I modeled?

Why This Matters Now

Year-end isn't just a deadline; it's a hinge point. Decisions you make now ripple into next year and beyond. This month is your chance to close out the year with intention—not just a quick gift, but a meaningful move. By aligning your giving with your goals, your values get carried forward, not just your wealth.

When you give intentionally and plan smarter, you don't just donate. You live your legacy.

WEEK 1

Strategic Giving—From The Heart & The Head

For many of us, giving feels personal. We donate because we care, because something moved us, or because it feels like the right thing to do. And that's good. Giving should come from the heart.

But when we pause to pair that emotional generosity with intentional financial planning, something powerful happens: We can increase the impact of our gifts—both for the causes we care about and for our own financial wellbeing.

This week, we explore how to give with both compassion and clarity. We'll walk through how to make giving part of your broader financial plan, evaluate causes that align with your values, and understand the timing and tools that can make your dollars stretch further.

Balancing Heartfelt Giving With Smart Strategy

Generosity doesn't need to be reactive. Instead of just responding to requests or donating on a whim in December to meet tax deadlines, imagine giving with a plan—one that aligns with your budget, values, and goals.

Start by asking yourself:

- *What causes or communities do I care most about?*
- *How much can I give this year without compromising my other financial goals?*
- *What's the best way to make my gift go further—for me and for the organization?*

When giving is intentional, it becomes part of your legacy, not just a transaction.

Give Where It Matters To You

Not all charities are created equal. That doesn't mean some are bad—but it does mean some are better aligned with your values than others.

To evaluate causes and organizations:

- Look for transparency and impact reporting.
- Consider whether you want to support large institutions or grassroots efforts.
- Use tools like GuideStar, Charity Navigator, or GiveWell to assess credibility.

And remember: *values-aligned giving* doesn't always have to mean formal charities. Helping a neighbor, supporting a local artist, or backing a community initiative can be just as meaningful.

Timing, Method, And The Mechanics Of Giving

Here's where strategy really comes into play. A $10,000 gift isn't always just a $10,000 gift. It can be much more powerful (and tax-efficient) when structured the right way.

Consider These Strategies:

- **Appreciated Securities:** Instead of giving cash, donate long-held stocks or mutual funds that have increased in value. You avoid capital gains tax and get a deduction for the full market value.
- **Bunching Donations:** If you're close to the standard deduction threshold, consider consolidating several years' worth of giving into one year to maximize your deduction.

- **Year-End Timing:** Making your gift before December 31st can secure a deduction for this tax year—but don't wait until the last week to plan.
- **Recurring Giving:** Setting up automatic monthly or quarterly donations helps you stay consistent and helps nonprofits manage their cash flow better.

Charitable Tools To Explore

As your giving becomes more structured, so can the tools you use:

- **Donor-Advised Funds (DAFs):** Think of a DAF like a charitable investment account. You contribute assets (cash, stocks, etc.), get an immediate tax deduction, and then decide over time how to grant the money out. It's great for bunching, long-term giving, or teaching children about philanthropy.
- **Qualified Charitable Distributions (QCDs):** If you're over age 70½, you can give directly from your IRA to a qualified charity without it counting as taxable income. (The maximum QCD amount is indexed for inflation each year, so check the IRS for the current limit.) A QCD is especially useful if you don't itemize deductions.
- **Charitable Remainder Trusts and Charitable Lead Trusts:** These more advanced strategies allow you to provide income to yourself or others now, with a charitable gift later—or vice versa. They combine generosity with estate and tax planning.

Final Thought

Giving isn't just about the money—it's about meaning. When you align your giving with your goals and use the right tools, your generosity becomes a legacy, not just a line item.

So this week, pause and reflect: what causes move you? What values do you want to support? And how can your giving be both heartfelt and high impact?

Action Step:

Choose one charitable giving strategy—like donating appreciated stock, using a DAF, or setting up a recurring gift—and implement it before year-end. Make a list of two to three causes that align with your values and research them with an eye toward impact and alignment.

WEEK 2

Donor-Advised Funds, Qualified Charitable Distributions, And Tax-Wise Giving

When it comes to charitable giving, good intentions are just the beginning. To make the biggest impact—for both the causes you care about and your own financial life—you also need strategy. This week is about using smart, tax-savvy tools to give more effectively.

Let's be clear: Generosity and smart planning aren't mutually exclusive. In fact, when you use the right giving vehicles, you can increase your giving power while reducing your tax burden. That's a win-win worth exploring.

Three Powerful Tools For Tax-Wise Giving

1. Donor-Advised Funds

A donor-advised fund is like a charitable investment account. You contribute to it, get an immediate tax deduction, and then recommend grants to your favorite charities over time.

Why DAFs are useful:

- You can "bunch" several years' worth of donations into one year for tax purposes—which is especially useful if you're close to the standard deduction threshold.
- You retain flexibility. You don't have to decide right away where the money goes; you can take your time.
- Investments in the DAF grow tax-free, potentially increasing your impact.

Example:

Let's say you normally give $5,000 a year to charity. If you bunch three years of gifts ($15,000) into a DAF this year, you could itemize your deduction in that high-giving year and take the standard deduction the next two years.

2. Qualified Charitable Distributions

QCDs allow individuals age 70½ or older to donate directly from their IRA to a qualified charity. These gifts count toward your Required Minimum Distributions (RMDs) and are excluded from your taxable income. These rules can change, so check with your advisor or the IRS.

Key rules:

• You must be at least 70½ years old.

• You can give up to $108,000 per year, per individual for 2025 — this amount is indexed for inflation, so check IRS.gov for the current year limit.

• The money must go directly from the IRA custodian to the charity.

• The recipient must be a qualified 501(c)(3) organization (not a donor-advised fund or private foundation).

Why QCDs matter:

- They lower your taxable income, which can reduce the tax on Social Security or Medicare premiums.
- They fulfill your RMD without increasing your tax bill.

Example:

If your RMD is $20,000 and you send $10,000 to a charity via a QCD, only the remaining $10,000 is taxable income. That can have a significant ripple effect on your overall tax picture.

3. Gifting Appreciated Stock

Instead of writing a check, you can gift appreciated securities (like stocks or mutual funds) directly to a charity.

Benefits:

- You avoid paying capital gains tax on the appreciation.
- You get a deduction for the full fair market value if you've held the asset for over a year.

Example:

You bought a stock for $2,000 that's now worth $10,000. If you sell it and donate the cash, you'll pay capital gains tax on $8,000. But if you donate the stock directly, you pay no capital gains—and deduct the full $10,000.

Timing and Planning Windows

Timing your giving can maximize the tax impact. Here's how to think about it:

- **During year-end reviews:** Evaluate whether you'll itemize or take the standard deduction and decide whether to bunch donations into a high-giving year.
- **Before RMDs:** If eligible, use QCDs before taking your full RMD.
- **During windfalls:** Big income years (e.g., selling a business, receiving a bonus) can be ideal for large contributions to DAFs or appreciated stock donations.

Final Thought

Charitable giving doesn't have to be reactive or last-minute. With tools like donor-advised funds, QCDs, and appreciated securities, you can make your generosity go further—for both the world and your wallet.

Action Step:

Review your current giving strategy. Are you writing checks or using tax-efficient tools? If you're over 70½, talk to your advisor about QCDs. If you hold appreciated assets, consider donating stock. And if you want long-term flexibility, look into opening a donor-advised fund.

WEEK 3

Giving As A Family Legacy

True legacy isn't just about money—it's about meaning. When you involve your children or grandchildren in your giving, you're not just making charitable contributions but are building a shared family story, passing on values, and creating traditions that last.

1. Involving Children And Grandchildren

Inviting younger generations into your giving decisions accomplishes two major things: it fosters empathy and ownership. You might begin by:

- Letting them pick one charity annually and match their contribution (you match $1 for every $2 they give).
- Having a "giving budget" portion of the family finances where they research and present charitable options.
- Creating a "junior board" or advisory role where each family member participates in how funds are granted.

These inclusive practices turn giving from a lecture into a legacy.

2. Passing On Values—Not Just Money

Money transferred without meaning often gets lost. Values give that money a direction. Consider asking:

- What values do we want to pass on? (service, justice,

the environment, education)

- How can our giving reflect those values year after year?
- How will we involve future generations in that value story?

You might write a **family giving vision statement** or create a short video that explains why you support certain causes—so your children understand *why* the dollars are going, not just *where*.

3. Building A Family Mission Around Philanthropy

A family mission brings coherence and identity to your collective giving. Some ideas:

- Pick a theme (e.g., "Education for All," "Local Community Resilience," "Healthcare Access").
- Establish a family fund or donor-advised fund that you review and decide on together each year.
- Hold an annual "giving review" where you evaluate last year's results and choose new initiatives.
- Create a physical symbol—a family giving tree, scrapbook, or simple certificate—to remind everyone of their shared mission.

This mission becomes more than charitable: It becomes part of your family's culture.

4. Practical Steps: Meetings, Funds, Traditions

- **Annual Giving Meeting:** Set a date each year (e.g., first Sunday in December) to gather your family, review giving results, share stories from recipients, and pick next year's focus.

- **Family Fund/DAF Setup:** Open a donor-advised fund in the family's name. Contribute annually, and let each member recommend grants under the fund's umbrella.
- **Giving Traditions**: Choose a recurring tradition—such as "Volunteer Day" each spring, "Charity Stock Gift" quarterly for each grandchild, or "Legacy Letter" writing for every major gift.
- **Education & Storytelling:** At each meeting, include a "cause spotlight" where one family member researches a charity and presents how the funds were used. Stories make giving real.

Final Thought

When you embed giving into your family's rhythm and involve the next generation, you create more than donations; you create identity, memory, and purpose. Your legacy isn't just the dollars you leave behind—it's the story you build together.

Action Step:

Schedule your first family giving meeting within the next 30 days. Define one shared philanthropic theme. Invite each child or grandchild to pick a cause and prepare a short presentation for the meeting.

WEEK 4

Reflect, Reassess, And Plan The Year Ahead

As the calendar turns, it's more than a new year—it's a new chapter. This week is dedicated to closing out the current year with intention, reviewing what worked (and what didn't), and setting clear goals for both your finances and your giving next year. Don't let December become a blur of receipts and last-minute gifts; instead, make it a launchpad for your next season. Use this time to start over next year with more clarity than the year before.

Closing The Year With Intention

Before the holiday lights fade and the tax bills arrive, take purposeful action:

- Review your budget and cash flow: Did you give the amount you intended? Did you save enough?
- Max out contributions where appropriate: 401(k)s, IRAs, HSAs, 529s. These deadlines matter.
- Make charitable gifts *before* December 31 to ensure they apply to this year's tax return.
- Take required minimum distributions (RMDs) if you're subject to them. Missing a deadline can trigger hefty penalties.
- Organize your receipts, donation letters, and investment statements so you're prepared for tax-season.

Closing intentionally means doing more than wrapping up—it means tying a bow on the year you've lived and learned.

Checklist: Contributions, Gifts, & Distributions

You've come a long way this year. Before the calendar turns, here are the practical steps that will lock in your progress:

- Reach or exceed your employer retirement plan contribution limit
- Make catch-up contributions if eligible (age 50+)
- Max out your HSA (if applicable)
- Review 529 contributions and front-load if desired
- Make charitable donations and obtain acknowledgments
- Make QCDs (if eligible) or other year-end charitable planning
- Take RMDs or evaluate withdrawals where needed
- Update your beneficiary designations and trust documents
- Verify that your estate and giving plans still reflect your current goals and life stage
- Back up documentation and ensure your giving and financial practices mirrored your values

Review What Worked—And What Didn't

A financial plan isn't static. It's a living document. Use this moment to ask yourself:

- Which financial habits helped me get closer to my goals? Which ones held me back?
- Did my giving reflect my values and bring satisfaction —not just tax relief?
- Did I involve my family in the ways I hoped?
- Were there expenses, tax surprises, or giving outcomes I didn't anticipate?
- Does my risk profile or time horizon feel different now?

Your honest review becomes the input for next year's strategy. Without it, you're simply repeating the same patterns in the hope of different results.

Setting Goals: One Financial, One Giving

With clarity from your review, let's establish two meaningful goals for next year: one for your finances, one for your giving.

Financial Goal

➡ *Example*: Increase my 401(k) contribution rate by two percentage points; reduce high-interest debt by 50%; or build 12 months of emergency savings.

- Make it specific, measurable, and time-bound.

Giving Goal

➡ *Example*: Establish a donor-advised fund and contribute $10,000; involve my kids in two giving decisions; or create a recurring monthly donation to a cause that reflects our family mission.

- Make it meaningful and connected to your values.

Write both goals down. Share them with a loved one or your advisor. Revisit them quarterly, not just at year-end.

Final Thought

Year-end excellence isn't about perfection—it's about alignment. It's not about trying to fix everything at once; it's about making one intentional decision today that shifts your story tomorrow.

By reflecting honestly, reassessing thoughtfully, and planning deliberately, you turn December from a backlog into a springboard.

Action Step:

Set aside one hour this week, grab your calendar and financial statements, and walk through the review questions. Then choose and write your two goals—financial and giving—for next year. Schedule a reminder in March to revisit them.

Wherever you are in this journey — just starting, mid-course, or looking back with more clarity than you had when you began — I hope this year has brought you closer to the life you actually want. Not the life on paper. The real one. Stay wealthy, healthy, and happy.

Client Convos: The Joy of Giving

One of my favorite clients — and I've had the privilege of many — is a couple who comes in for their annual review and asks me the same question every time: how much can we give away this year?

For most clients, that question is about vacations, or a home renovation, or something for the grandchildren. For them, it's always about their charitable work. They're deeply involved with an organization — on the board, in the operations, in the mission. It's not a line item in their plan. It's the point of the plan.

At some point, their passion became contagious. I got involved too. I've shown up, volunteered, helped out. Because when you see clients who have built a financial life with this kind of clarity of purpose — not just what they have, but what it's for — it changes how you think about everything we do in this work. That's what financial planning is supposed to be, at its best: not just wealth managed, but a life lived on purpose.

CLOSING CHAPTER

More Than a Plan—A Partnership for Life

I've been sitting across tables from people for over twenty years now. Young couples scared to look at their own bank accounts. Business owners who'd built everything and hadn't thought once about what came next. Parents who wanted to give their kids everything and didn't know how to give them the right things. In every single conversation, money was the least interesting part. What mattered was always the life underneath it — the fears, the hopes, the people they loved and wanted to protect. This book is my attempt to put those conversations on paper. I hope it's been useful. More than that, I hope it's been honest.

You've made it to the end—but really, this is just the beginning.

This book was never meant to be a replacement for a financial advisor. It's a conversation starter, a guide to help you get clear on what matters most to you so you can move forward with purpose and confidence. Financial planning isn't a one-and-done checklist. It's an evolving process, just like life itself.

So, now what?

What To Look For In A Financial Advisor

The right advisor can serve as a guide, coach, and accountability partner. But finding that right fit takes intention. It's not about choosing the firm with the fanciest brochures or the most impressive titles. It's about trust, relationship, and values alignment.

Look for someone who:

- Listens more than they talk
- Asks questions that go beyond dollars and cents
- Understands your values and life goals
- Has a team that can support you through life's seasons
- Has access to resources and tools that can grow with you

Fit matters. Culture matters. If it doesn't feel right, it probably isn't. A good advisor relationship should make you feel safe, motivated, and heard.

Good advisors don't just help you organize your money. They help you build a life that feels purposeful, steady, and deeply your own. When your financial plan reflects your values and supports your happiness, you're not just preparing for what comes next. You're giving yourself room to live fully right now.

Here's to a future built with intention, clarity, and joy.

The Future Of Financial Planning

There's always a new tool or trend on the horizon: apps, AI, algorithms. And while technology will continue to improve how we gather and analyze financial data, it can't replace the human side of planning.

Because the best financial plans don't start with numbers—

they start with stories.

Your story. Your family. Your dreams. Your fears.

And the right advisor doesn't just build a portfolio; they build a partnership. They ask: *What's most important to you? What keeps you up at night? What kind of legacy do you want to leave?*

The future of financial planning is deeply human, built on empathy, trust, and shared understanding. Technology can crunch numbers, but only people can hold your hand through hard decisions.

Accountability, Motivation, And The Power Of Relationship

One of the most underestimated benefits of having a financial advisor? Accountability.

Life gets busy. Plans fall to the side. But an advisor helps you keep the promises you've made to yourself and your family. They encourage you when you feel stuck. They re-center you when emotions run high. They help you stay the course when the world feels uncertain.

Because let's be honest: Sometimes what we need most isn't just advice. It's someone to remind us why we started and what we're working toward.

That's where the magic happens. That's where planning becomes more than numbers—it becomes life alignment.

It's Not Just Financial Planning. It's Life Planning.

If there's one idea I hope you walk away with, it's this: your financial life is about far more than money.

It's about how you live, what you value, and who you love.

At its core, planning is about balance. A life built on discipline but devoid of joy isn't a life well-lived—and a life full of joy without structure often creates stress. Advisors don't just help you accumulate wealth; they help you craft a financial life that supports happiness, adventure, rest, and meaning. The goal isn't to work endlessly. It's to create a life where you can confidently say yes to the things that matter most.

Whether you're just starting your journey or revisiting a plan you made years ago, remember that financial planning is an ongoing process. It evolves as you do. The right plan—built with the right partner—will reflect not just where you are, but where you want to go and *why* you want to go there.

So ask yourself: Who's helping me make those decisions? Who's walking alongside me?

Find someone who doesn't just know the rules of finance, but knows how to ask the right questions. Someone who sees you, not just your assets.

And most importantly, someone who believes what I believe: **Financial planning isn't just about money. It's about living the life you want—on purpose.**

Stay Wealthy, Healthy, and Happy.

AUTHOR'S NOTE

A Note of Thanks

Dear Reader,

Thank you for spending this year with me.

Writing this book was an act of hope — hope that the right words, at the right moment, might help someone make a better decision, have a harder conversation, or simply feel less alone in navigating their financial life.

If this book has been useful to you, I have one small ask.

Tell someone about it.

Word of mouth is how books like this find the people who need them most. If something in these pages resonated — a story, a framework, a question you hadn't thought to ask — share it. Recommend it to a friend, a family member, a colleague who's been putting off the hard conversations. Leave a review on Amazon or wherever you purchased it. Even a sentence or two makes an enormous difference.

You can find me at diversifiedllc.com, where my team and I write regularly about the same topics we've covered here — and where we'd be glad to help you take the next step. I'd love to have you sign up for my blog there, or to follow along on social.

Thank you for reading. Thank you for sharing. And as always — ***Stay Wealthy, Healthy, and Happy.***

— Andrew Rosen, CFP®

ACKNOWLEDGEMENT

This book is the result of countless conversations over the years—conversations with clients, colleagues, and friends who have trusted me with their stories, their goals, and their concerns. I'm deeply grateful to the individuals and families who have allowed me to be part of their financial lives. Your experiences and perspectives have shaped the ideas in these pages more than anything else.

I'm especially grateful to Sarah Thomas for her invaluable editing, insight, and support throughout the development of this book. Her ability to help shape, refine, and elevate these ideas was instrumental in bringing this project to life. This book would not be what it is without her contributions.

To the team at Diversified LLC, thank you for your commitment to thoughtful planning and for continually raising the standard of what financial advice can be. It's a privilege to work alongside professionals who care deeply about the people we serve.

I'm also thankful to the mentors and peers who have influenced my thinking over the years. Your guidance and perspective have helped shape my approach to both planning and life.

And finally, to my family—thank you for your support, patience, and encouragement throughout this process. You are the foundation that makes everything else possible.

ABOUT THE AUTHOR

Andrew Rosen

Andrew Rosen, CFP® is the Executive Chairman of Diversified, a national wealth management firm overseeing more than $3.5 billion in assets. A CFP® professional and Certified Estate Planner, Andrew is known for his thoughtful, human-centered approach to financial planning, helping individuals and families align their money with what matters most. With over two decades of experience, his work focuses on behavioral decision-making, retirement planning, and designing financial lives built on clarity and intention. Andrew is a frequent contributor to Forbes and Kiplinger and speaks nationally on intentional financial planning and advisor leadership.

FOR MORE INFORMATION

If you found this book helpful and want to take the next step...

Visit: diversifiedllc.com

To connect with our team and begin building your own intentional financial plan.

YOUR INTENTIONAL FINANCIAL LIFE

www.ingramcontent.com/pod-product-compliance
Lightning Source LLC
LaVergne TN
LVHW040218110826
845146LV00005B/1335

* 9 7 9 8 9 9 5 7 7 5 7 1 3 *